An Offering of Words

An Offering of Words

Homilies

Monsignor Robert P. Hundt

LaScala Publishing
Montgomery Village, Maryland

Dedicated to the Blessed Sacrament faith family
of La Crosse, Wisconsin

Publisher's Note: These homilies were originally offered in Blessed Sacrament Parish and in area churches within the Diocese of La Crosse, Wisconsin. Many of the author's original *speaker's marks,* and much of the *layout form and special punctuation* used in the original compositions have been retained herein.

Published in the United States by LaScala Publishing
Post Office Box 87403, Montgomery Village, Maryland 20886-7403

ISBN 0-9747159-1-3

Cover Design: Sandra L. Wester

Cover Art – Stained glass window designed and painted by Joep Nicolas. At the time this particular work was installed at Blessed Sacrament Church in 1949, Nicolas was considered to be the "father of modern stained glass" in America. Window fabrication and installation by Rambusch Company, New York and New Jersey.

Contents

Foreword

Father Hundt has written *another* love story. This time, for the most part, it's about Blessed Sacrament Parish and of all those who dwell therein. Never in my most sincere prayer did I imagine that one day I would receive a call from La Crosse asking me to help that *love story* find its way to the printed page.

The Great Jubilee Year 2000 was cause for great celebration in all of Christianity. Holy Mother Church, under the careful guidance of John Paul II, helped each one of us mark this occasion with special liturgies, ceremonies, Eucharistic convocations and other prayerful activities. Our participation in these events indelibly etched on our souls the fact that we were witnesses of the beginning of the Third Millennium of Christianity.

It was in the midst of this time that I had my first *personal* visit to Blessed Sacrament Parish in La Crosse. A previous encounter, where I helped a priest-friend from Washington, D.C. make his way there to offer a Sunday of Sermons in the parish, planted the seed for the visit I made in the year 2000.

I had asked my La Crosse friends if I could attend Mass with them during my brief weekend visit, after which I was presented with a remembrance gift: A book of their Pastor's Homilies. On my flight home to Maryland I began to read what I would later tell my wife was "the most beautiful love story I had ever read."

Knowing that I was a perpetual student of homiletic writings, my wife asked for more on my discovery. I explained that "the homilies of this parish priest in Wisconsin are about his people, his flock. Sure, he brings every important element of our faith into his sermons, but there are stories of the land, the people, of life, its challenges and it's all tied back into the *Truth*."

And so began my long-distance relationship with this priest-homilist I had yet to meet. Re-reading the homilies of that first book drew me closer to Father Hundt's place on earth, his people, their practice of faith, and nearer to the *love* that surely flourished where this priest provided guidance.

When the opportunity presented itself to again visit La Crosse, this time to tour and experience the magnificent Shrine of Our Lady of Guadalupe, I quickly moved everything aside. Once again my hosts provided a stop at Blessed Sacrament Church, suggesting I needed to see how the main altar renovations were coming along. Such love for their parish. The kind of love that Fr. Hundt taught me about in his book of homilies, received on my first visit.

As we entered the church on Losey Boulevard, all lights were out, allowing the remaining sunlight of the day to beam through the magnificent stained glass windows around the perimeter of the space. Until our eyes adjusted to the light, the windows demanded our attention as it does now in this current offering of words from Father, now Monsignor, Hundt.

An Offering of Words uses the stained glass, sacred art to demand our attention, in a gentle way, as our eyes and hearts begin to adjust and focus on the first homily and the light Christ provides.

Be Filled With The Life Of Christ clearly establishes who Monsignor Hundt knows to be most important in everyone's walk of faith. We are then treated to a glimpse of Blessed Sacrament's Pastor in his first Sunday Mass. There are sermons celebrating the Mother of God, Her Son, the gospel messages, the priesthood, family, the sacraments and the lives of parishioners.

As the reader continues, one can not help but notice that what appears on the page is quite different from most other volumes of creative work. Monsignor Hundt composes his original homilies using felt-tip pen and paper. When transcribing to the type-written page, this *diagrammatic* style of the original homilies is maintained as much as possible--- to preserve the poetic nature of what and how he writes.

It is this precise poetic style that helps the *reader* of his homilies actually hear the voice of the author coming from the pulpit. For parishioners, it's possible to relive the moments when they first heard these words, to once again grab-hold of the messages, the lessons, the richness of what Monsignor Hundt shared then and shares now.

Blessed are we all to have lived during the time of Pope John Paul II. In the tribute to this Holy Father (*Into Your Hands I Commend My Suffering*), there is unique treatment given to the formation of words on the first page. This image is merely a shadow of the impact one life can have on teaching the world about suffering, as Jesus was certainly the Pontiff's model throughout his life.

As the portrait of American life and spiritual guidance continues through the readings, many are the times when even if you know none of those mentioned, tears find their way to your cheeks as you grieve with the families and loved ones who remain as *Church Militant.*

How fitting that the final homily offering is *Little Tabernacles.* Truly the *beginning*, this beautiful chapter in Monsignor Hundt's love story offers a spotlight back onto all homilies that came before it.

These offerings are not intended to be absorbed in a single reading. The physical placement of words on the page facilitates a methodical intake of the phrases that teach, soothe, guide, urge, encourage and offer hope. They are meant to be read slowly, with care, one or two homilies at a sitting.

When taken as a body of work, this effort demonstrates a certain Christ-like quality, which Jesus the Carpenter must have learned from St. Joseph. Start with material that is *true*, and from that, all else that happens becomes *True.*

Clear, plain, bold, creative, concise and beautiful---asking all of us to implore Him, "Lord, stay with us."

Rus Wester

Preface

This is an unusual book. The only way the author will know what is found between its covers is to read the book, just as you are poised to do.

Blessed Sacrament parishioners urged this book. Homily titles and selection were done by parishioners. Several of them typed and archived the homilies. The parish is providing for the production costs. The parish will benefit from any profits that may be realized. The parish literally owns this book.

What the author owns and can't deny, for better or worse, is the content. It is rather scary and challenging to put one's homilies in printed form for public scrutiny and criticism. A homily is an intimate thing. It calls one to reveal deeper feelings about Church, Christ and the Christian life. Revealing feelings and personal thoughts about the deeper things of life make one vulnerable. But for the sake of those who wanted this effort, vulnerability will be accepted.

The title of the book was the author's idea. An idea not easily sold to the publisher, but he was marvelously helpful and accommodating in so many ways and accepting this title, "An Offering of Words" was one of them. A homily is, after all, "an offering of words" to be accepted or rejected by the listener or reader, but no matter what the reaction, it remains the author's offering---the best that could be done at a given moment.

I am delighted that these offerings have built up, consoled, challenged or encouraged people in their initial hearing. I am further delighted that these same words will also help build our Parish Center. If these words have helped our parish family in the present, then the Parish Center will help do the same for future generations yet to be born.

I wish to thank many people. Jim Altman, a seminarian of our parish, spent untold hours deciphering the author's handwriting and typing these homilies. Thanks to Barb Swieciak who also converted hand-written homilies into those you see here. Pauline Connell put together a team of homily manuscript readers and selectors, offered the titles for the work and was the "glue" that held our production and prayer teams together. Susan Fukuda was our project "gatekeeper" as she coordinated communications within the parish and kept me and the publisher on the same page. Allan Fukuda provided the beautiful photograph for the front cover.

Our list of manuscript readers and those offering prayers and special counsel for this endeavor looks like the litany of saints: Liz Nutter, Marie Allen, Herb Lee, Dorothy Lawrence, Helen and Bill Mackey, Mary Noelke, Steve and Marian Pavela, Rev. John Potaczek, Mary Ann Bradley, Irene Chojnacki and the Franciscan Sisters at the Villa St. Joseph. Thanks also to Sandy Wester for her care in guiding the editorial process for the book, and her husband for providing its foreword.

Thanks also to Tom and Anne Gees who worked tirelessly on a number of aspects of this book. In their offering a gift of earlier homilies to friends in Maryland, LaScala Publishing became the most enthusiastic promoter of this project.

To those who generously subsidized this effort, my most sincere thanks.

For those whom I may have forgotten, I offer an old man's memory as the culprit. Finally, I have to thank all of you who will find a good and worthy exercise in accepting "An Offering of Words" into your lives…once again.

May God Bless You Abundantly,

Msgr. Robert P. Hunlt

November 10, 2005

Feast of Pope St. Leo the Great

Be Filled with the Light of Christ

There is a German folktale about an aging father who had three sons.
One day he told them:
"The one who fills the barn to capacity today will inherit the farm."
The oldest son rushed to fill the barn with all the cows,

> a couple of horses,
> three goats and
> a flock of chickens
> But, there was still room in the barn.

It was noon – the barn was emptied and the second son began filling the barn with hay.
But there was still empty space in the barn.
By the time the barn was emptied for the third son it was already dark

> All he had was a little candle that he had made.
> He put it in the center of the barn and lit it.

Standing outside, the father could see no empty spaces through the windows and cracks. Light was spilling out into the darkness.

> The barn was filled with light in every corner.

The father gave the farm to the youngest son.
The youngest son did the least work and filled the barn.
The emptiness was filled with light.
Does this say something to us about Christ being light to the world?
It is said that many people feel that this life is empty.
It's meaningless-
No purpose-darkness-depression-dull sadness…a sense that there must be more.
I assure you, dear friends, there is more, so much more.
And we don't ever need to work to find the "more".
We need to quit trying to fill the emptiness with material things…
Projects--- Careers
We need to be like the stable in Bethlehem…

Empty
Humble
Unimportant

That was the place the light of the world was to be born and the humble place was filled

With highs
With eternal riches
With joy
With the hope, of the Lord

Some one could say: Oh Lord, that seems pretty imaginative.

I want some practical stuff.
I can't see any importance.
I can't see Christ in what you are saying
In fact, I can't see Christ in what you do
around the altar.

I want to see Christ, show me Christ.

The Gospel says blessed are the pure of heart, they shall see God.
The pure of heart hear the word of the sacred scriptures as truly
the Word of God.
The pure of heart truly see Christ's presence in the consecrated
bread and wine.
The pure of heart see that they truly must be pure of heart to receive
Holy Communion.
The pure of heart, like the good woman we buried some weeks ago,
see the angels and saints that surround our altar when mass is being
celebrated.
The pure of heart see that they are present both at the Lord's Supper
and at Calvary as we make present the One saving us all---Christ.
The pure of heart have their minds and spirits filled with the light
which is Christ.
They can see Christ here just barely hidden behind the bread and the
wine.

The actions at the altar…
The spoken word of the sacred scriptures…

Blessed are the clear of heart for they shall see God.
The clear of heart – Humble ---Quiet---Trusting---Child-like
are the foolish of the world who shame the wise.
The weak who shame the strong.

Those who count for nothing, who are reduced to nothing,
those who are something of the world, judge things.
So many try to fill the house of their souls and spirits with too many
material things.
While only the light of Christ will truly fill it.
Fill it to the point where the light spills out into works of
> Charity
> Faith
> Happy Marriage
> Honest and Just Business Practices
> Volunteerism

Generous to others with their gifts to church and other charities.
Blessed are they, the beatitudes tell us, who reach for the very best
they can be.
Blessed are they who are never apathetic or satisfied with a minimum.
Blessed are they who see that the only true and lasting catastrophe of life
is to be less than a saint.
Blessed are they who fill the house of their life with the light
which is Christ.

Some day that light will be joined to the light of Christ in the church
of heaven
> Of which the word of God says,
> There is no light in that city because Christ is the Light.

Let me see Christ – now.

Blessed are the pure of heart they shall see God – now.

Corpus Christi

What you see is what you get...You may conclude I'm windy but I did not bring the tornado warning.
I come to you today with some fear,
                much excitement
                and much hope.
My **fears** I hope are ungrounded and
mostly fear vanishes when I tell myself I do not need to
look after this large and grand enterprise alone.

                I remind myself that Blessed Sacrament Parish
                is renowned for the quantity and quality of it's
                volunteer help and **lay leadership**.
                I remind myself that I come to you firstly as a **priest**.
                        One who presides at baptisms
                                        weddings
                                        funerals
                                        confessions
        and most especially to preside at the sacrifice of the Mass.

I remind myself of the **Words Christ**
spoken so often to his disciples,
the three word sentence our Holy Father
constantly repeats and exhorts us to heed.
                        That short phrase is:

                        "Be not afraid."

With all those reminders firmly in place my fear of coming to you
as your priest and your pastor, subside.
I am fully aware that I come to you as successor to great leaders like
Msgr. Wagener and **Fr. McGarty**. Each had their gifts which they
shared with you so fully. Each has left his **mark**, his **flavor** on the
family of Blessed Sacrament.
I hope only to preserve all the good they have left and by God's grace
over the years leave a faint flavor of my own.

I hope I come to you blessed with your initial trust.
I pledge to you I will always try to be worthy of that trust.
I come to you with **excitement.**
As every new challenge brings it's component of excitement
  I share with you a major reason for my excitement.
  Your wonderful dedication to Catholic education expressed
  so powerfully through your school and your commitment to
  Aquinas schools.
  I assure you I will in every way possible
  support and encourage the continuing excellence of
  Blessed Sacrament school and Aquinas schools.

I come to you at Blessed Sacrament knowing some of you well---
Right off hand, I can tell you I have four aunts, an uncle, my Godparents,
a niece and her husband and grandnephews.
And... likely many people I know well or not so well, whom I didn't
even know were part of Blessed Sacrament.
I also have many friends and acquaintances I've met over the years who
all are among the great family of Blessed Sacrament.
I come to you with **hope**---That hope is not founded on my gifts
          talents
          energy or
          enthusiasm.
They are minimal to be sure.
My hope is grounded rather on Christ, human life and heart,
and through the Bishop.
Christ the Lord of history and of every human life and heart
has brought us together.
His injunction to me and to you is the same:
       "Be faithful to Me."

I will try to be faithful to the Lord and His saving truth
and in that way, I can be faithful to you.
I will attempt to bring to your attention and mine the fullness
 of the gospel:
      *the consoling and the challenging
      *the encouraging and the condensing
        Word of God.
We have **our first Sunday together on the Feast of Corpus Christi**.
I take it as a good omen.

I notice the beautiful rose window in the back of the church with the
wheat and the grapes and at this end we
have real wheat and real wine--- we are
enveloped in the Eucharist.
Around the altar table we celebrate Christ's sacrifice.
As we begin the process of knitting together a new pastor with
a parish long established.......
Let us remember the primary knitting project each of us has is to knit our
life with Christ. The primary place for that knitting process is here
around the altar of sacrifice where we hear Christ tell us over and again:
"This is My body, My blood,
My life, My everything for you."
Consider the wonder of that moment long ago.
Christ literally held His life in His hands and said:
"Here, My life is My gift to you."
Each time the Holy Sacrifice is offered, that wonder is repeated for you
and for me.
I will tell you most honestly, dear people---
Nothing Blessed Sacrament parish can offer thrills me more deeply and
consistently than the privilege of standing at the altar and repeating the

powerful,
redeeming,
creative words of Christ;
The most splendid words in all of history and I hope that His words do
not sound hollow in my mouth.

**For I want those words to speak not only of Christ's gift to us
but also of my gift to you.**

"Here I am, this is my life, my energy
my love for you."
Here especially we are knit together
as one family
as priest and people
sharing one same self-giving, redeeming Lord.
As we pray in Eucharistic prayer III
Grant that we,
who are nourished by his Body and Blood
may be filled with his Holy Spirit
and become one body, one spirit in Christ.

Father Apfelbeck's 1st Mass

I come to you in fear and trembling.
A very formidable man has given me strict orders…
    several times repeated.
He told me exactly what my effort is **not** to be and
    how **long** it **is** to be.

My words are not to be about a man but about the Gospel…
and my words are not to exceed 10 minutes.
That formidable man may get his first request.

So gingerly and with much trepidation I greet
and applaud Fr. Kurt Apfelbeck in these first hours
during which he is properly and rightly addressed
with the greatest title any man can claim - the title "Father".

I thank you Father Apfelbeck for allowing me this special privilege
and honor. I want to commend and applaud your <u>parents</u>, Father,
who have given, this day, not one, but, **two** sons to the Church.

Mr. and Mrs. Apfelbeck, your sons will never give you
grandchildren in the Apfelbeck blood line but, they will give you
hundreds, even thousands in the royal blood line
of Christ the King and Savior and Lord.

            And both in this life and in the halls of eternity
            those spiritual grandsons and granddaughters born
            to you through the service of your priest sons
            will hold the two of you in wonder and high esteem.

The Gospel today is rich and wonderfully appropriate for the moment we
celebrate. The Gospel is about free and radical choice,
                            free and deliberate choice
                        which goes to the root of our lives.
Choices which touch the roots can be most uncomfortable,
as anyone who has ever had a dental root canal operation can testify.
This day has touched the life giving roots of the family

in parents
and sons.

There is a vast body of opinion loose in our society
which would call this day an exercise in foolishness and irrelevancy.
So many would say, how foolish to give up the prospects of
      wife and children,
      a lucrative career and travel,
      nice home and fine cars.

The words of the Gospel, which call on us to love God
even beyond father or mother, sons or daughters
were spoken by the One who was judged so irrelevant in His day
that they hung Him on a cross.

Those who thought they had all the relevant--- significant--- meaningful
modern facts and new-age trends clearly in mind are remembered only
because the One they put to death to quiet both Him and the mob
rose from the dead totally undoing the plan
                        and the work of the worldly wise
                        politically correct
                        relevant schemers...

Those famous characters of history... Pontius Pilate, Caiaphas,
Herod, Judas
would be known to none except for the relevant, crowd pleasing action
they decided upon turned out to be illuminated by the great light that
shines from the empty tomb of the eternal Son of God. Their relevant,
self-satisfying, popular decision was revealed to be tragically and
eternally wrong.

Today you have chosen to be a radical Christian but really there can be
no other kind as the Gospel today tells us.
The radical Christian man or woman, priest or lay person
is the manner of person who will forever be judged an irrelevant trouble
                        maker or foolish, impractical
                        dreamer.
Yet, what an honor---what a dignity--- what a joy
To be judged worthy to fall into the same category of uselessness as
the crucified Lord.
I say to our new priest today what I would say to every new priest and
every Catholic Christian.

Dare to be irrelevant.
Dare to speak and live eternal truths.
Dare to be called an impractical dreamer.
Dare this even when the reaction of many reduces you to frustration,
                          confusion,
                          discouraged sadness or silence.
In such moments, and surely they will come,
recall the words of Christ, your Teacher and Master, when He said:
                     "Come to Me, you who labor and are
                     burdened and I will refresh you."

I say to our new priest, dare to preach objective truth to a world drunk on
subjective desires.
Dare to preach the power of self denial to a world growing weak
            with self-gratification.
Dare to preach the gift of salvation to a world convinced
            it can save itself.
Dare to preach the value of the God given gift of life from conception
            to natural death to a world infatuated with cynical
            engineering of both conception and death.
Dare to preach the courage and freedom of obedience to a world
            convinced obedience is the virtue of whimps.
Dare to preach the dignity of humility to a world in love with the moral
            puberty called self-esteem.

Dare to preach the total Gospel---
                the cross as well as the Resurrection
                the consoling Word of God, as well as, the condemning
                the mercy and the justice
                the agony and the ecstasy
                the martyrdom and the victory.
Dare to preach the wondrous freedom of purity of mind and body
to a world which treats sex as no more than a handy tool of recreation.
Dare to preach the total glorious richness of the Catholic Creed.
Dare to preach the sturdy bracing wealth of the crown jewel of
Catholicism, which is the treasury of teaching
the moral rights and wrongs.
Dare to speak of the power hidden in the desire to do as we ought
and the weakness in the desire to do only what we wish.

9

Dare to do these things, Fr. Apfelbeck. You will then be judged by many to be irrelevant, old fashioned, lacking in sensitivity, foolish, too young to be taken seriously and just a bit quaint.

It may well seem a kind of death and certainly it will be your cross.
But remember it is the cross Christ fitted to you
This very day, the day you chose and were found fit to share
in the total life of a crucified priest who was the wisdom
and the eternal Truth of man and God in the flesh,
our Savior and Lord...

This day is the beginning of irrelevancy for a world closed on itself but, also the day you are empowered to open the fountains of God's mercy to all who seek true fulfillment in Life.

Finally the task of every Catholic Christian, priest or lay person is not to convince others of the truths of our faith but firstly,
to convince ourselves of this wonder of divine power and love and wisdom, which is our Catholic heritage.
If with God's grace we truly convince ourselves then we will live as a new creation. A new person in a society growing old and frail and weak because of over reliance on purely human wisdom.

Finally, the only thing which will convince the world of Christ's power and the eternal
>
> unchanging
> and
> saving

Truths of Christ are those Truths enfleshed, incarnate in our life style.

Fr. Kurt-you have chosen a life which
among so many is considered irrelevant
>
> useless
> politically incorrect.

Remember, they too are people to whom you must minister.
Only your holiness of life, your purity of motive, your constancy of intent will open a path to their hearts.

You will stand at the altar daily, there to repeat Christ's words,

>
> this is My life

> My body
> My love
> My blood
> My everything for you.

If you make these words your own then truly you have made the radical choice for Christ. But, also see those self-same words as your gift to the people to whom you minister.

> my people-this is my body
> my blood
> my energy
> my life for you

This will insure that you will fill the halls of heaven with a multitude of your spiritual sons and daughters---

> for the glory of God
> the honor of the Church
> the joy of your parents and
> the guarantee of your salvation.

Donna Voiku's Funeral

First of all this morning a word of consolation and sympathy to Dan---
Joseph---Matthew

> sister, Barbara--- brother, George

> Thelma and George - Donna's parents, Jon- a nephew,
> Christine and Susan – nieces

> Students of Matthew's 4th grade class at Blessed Sacrament
> Students of Joseph's sophomore class at Aquinas

All friends.

My guess is that more than a few of you have walked the street named
Via Veneto in Rome.

It's a street on which one finds over-priced boutiques and restaurants,
sidewalk cafes filled with tourists, the American Embassy.

You have only moved up the street a couple hundred feet when you have
already passed a small church named Santa Maria de Concezione.
St. Mary of the Conception.

In that Church, at the base of the street which glitters with the finest
clothes, jewelry, food and cars that human genius has devised, is a
somber reminder of the great reality we try to deny.

As you enter the crypt of the church you
notice over the door these words:

> "What **you are** we once were.
> What we **are** you shall be"

Then you step through the door and you see hundreds of skeletons,
human bones arranged in floral like displays, piles of grinning human
skulls, pull chains on lamps made of human bones.
The noise outside of commerce and vacationers, horns blowing,

motorinos screeching is very muted - **inside there is hardly a whisper.**

> Some linger and stare in shocked silence,
> some hurry away.
> Some clearly are plunged into deep thought.
> **Everyone** has forgotten the glitzy Via Veneto.

T. S. Elliot said:
> **"Humankind can not bear very much reality."**

But reality eventually cuts through every defense we put in its way.

Even the most secure defense is ultimately breached by death.

Donna visited Rome. If she visited this church, with the spirit
with which I knew her,
I believe this good and faithful woman would have appreciated the
delicious humor of this reminder
of our destiny on the most glamorous street of all of Rome.

She would have brought her profound Catholic Christian faith to the
scene. She would have inwardly reflected on the **swift** passing of time,
the **uncertainty** of life and the saintly procession of all these
boney monks into the light beyond the dark night of death.

She would not have merely gawked. She would have prayed.

As many of you know: "Donna means "lady" in Italian.
Donna was truly a "lady": dignified, cultured,
> always courteous & respectful, gracious
> gentle,
> noble of bearing, bright,
> intelligent far beyond the average,
> smiling,
> warm & loving in
a way that was never cloying or embarrassing.
Donna was loyal, as befits the daughter of a U.S. Marine Major.

"Semper Fidelis" - "Always Faithful," humble, responsible devotion to
> duty prompted this beautiful lady, this Donna, to put aside
> professional career & continuing education when Joseph and
> Matthew were infants, toddlers & early grade-schoolers.
She devoted herself to the greatest calling a woman can know...

she devoted herself to being a **mother** to her sons,
and a devoted wife to you Dan.
Upon you she conferred the greatest title
a man can possibly achieve in this life
> She made you **"Father"** of
> two splendid boys.

Someone once asked the author Henry James this question:
> "Do tell me, what do you think of life?"

> **"I think"**, replied the author,
> **"it is a predicament which precedes death."**

Life truly is a predicament and a bitter joke if all there is, is death.

> A cause for **despair** if all the love
> > all the caring
> > all the genius of medicine,
> > all the prayers,
> > all the longing for life

are finally reduced to nothing more than a day so bitter as today.

But life is so much more for the Christian believer.

Life is that privileged moment open to the possibility of coming to know
that life's total fulfillment is, by the human spirit's intuition and God's
loving design, truly out of this world.

Donna, the woman of faith, knew this.

She knew with St. Augustine "the human heart was made
> for God and will not rest until it rests in Him"

She who knew so many homes,
> > cities,
> > towns in her life
knew also with the writer of the Letter to the Hebrews:

"We seek the city that is to come - the heavenly Jerusalem"
She accepted with every fiber of her faith-filled spirit:

"On this mountain God has stripped away the veil
that veils all people - He has stripped away death."

This lady believed with all her humble faith-filled soul that
Just as Christ died
>   and rose to life again
>   so we who are baptized into Christ's death
>   will rise to new life.

She believed with all her reverent spirit that she actually held
Eternal Life on her tongue each time she received the Lord in
Holy Communion. For **Christ's** words were God's **Eternal
Truth to her.**

**"If you eat My Body & drink My Blood you have eternal life in
you."**

Donna was educated well beyond the average.
She walked easily and securely in the world of higher education.

But Donna's highest education was the work of the Holy Spirit and God's
revelation which blew the cap off a closed world and allowed her to see
into the heart and mind of an all-loving God.

To see into the realm of eternal glory where the great crowd of the
redeemed are gathered around the throne of the Lamb.

> Her highest education, the work of divine faith and the Holy
> Spirit allowed her to love and ponder the mysterious ways of
> God not attainable by human reason. Today we can hope that
> she no longer sees as through a dark glass but, face-to-face in
> an ecstasy of love and fulfillment which can never be dimmed
> or diminished.

"I must go to prepare a place for you" Jesus said
on the last night before His passion and death.
On that promise the believer supports a life of faith.
Our faith allows us to hope that this
>   wonderful mother, wife, daughter, sister,
>   friend now knows the place
>   Christ has prepared for those
>   who loved Him through the joys
>   and sorrows of life.

15

"I will not leave you orphans.

      I will be with you all days", is the promise
of our Divine Lord to all of us who grieve and are saddened today.

Donna went bravely and too soon into that dark night.

But our **faith** allows us to hope, our **charity** impels us to hope that the
dark night opened up to the glory and the eternal light of the Church of
Heaven.

The Church filled with human bones at the base of the Via Veneto is a
stark reminder of the predicament called life.

> But faith tells us that we are called to that City
> where streets are of pure gold, transparent as glass.
> where there is no temple in the City, the Lord, **God the**
>   **Almighty,** is its temple.
> The city has **no sun or moon** for the Glory of God gave it light
> and its Lamp was the Lamb.

Our faith allows us to hope Donna knows that City, the eternal
      Jerusalem, today.

> And finally, that faith is our consolation on
> the day of funeral.

How Holy the Family

When we finish with Christmas there is a letdown, a soft landing for most I hope, but still a letdown. We must fight against post holiday depression. After all, Christmas speaks of the beginning of new life, not the end of life.

Today we reflect that the child of Bethlehem was discovered by

Angels,
Shepherds,
Kings,
Worshiping kings
and
Murderous kings

In the context of a **family.**

With God all things are possible, the Sacred Scripture tells us.

So it was not **necessary**
that God come among us
as an infant
And
entrust himself to a human mother
and to Joseph, a foster father.

God didn't **need** to entrust Himself to two people
faced with the awesome task of caring for God's Son
and equipped only with the graces and gifts
that came to them because of their vocation
as a married couple.

God was not **bound** to that plan, **but He chose it!**

What awesome things that says about marriage
about family life.

Marriage must be very close to the heart of God.

Why do I say that?

Well, consider.

The **very first institution** that God put in place
at the dawning of creation
was the family.

Adam and Eve ---   the man
                        the woman
                                given to each other
                                as **gifts** from God.
In each other each found their **compliment**
and their **equal**
their **soul mate** and **confidant**
                            fully **equal**, but **different**
with a difference that made each of them
come fully and richly alive
in the presence of the other.

Already in the **second chapter of Genesis,** the very **beginning of the story of Salvation,** we have those beautiful words…man and wife
                     husband and wife,
                     and very soon mother, father, child.

So close to the heart of God is marriage and family that they appear immediately in the story of God's plan for humankind.

Marriage and family is the agency God employed to pass on
                          human life,
                          civilization
                          culture
                          and finally, **Salvation**

The story of Salvation which includes God's own birth into a human family could not have been written or accomplished without man and wife and family over all the generations that stretch from the dawn of history to the closing days of the 20th century.
                   Oh, it could have been **done another way**,
                   but **God chose** the family as the agency
                   through which it would be done,
                   and therefore all the other possibilities
                   must be considered…less good
                              less wise
                                less worthy
                                because the all wise
                                and good God
                                chooses that which is
                                truly best for us.

Consider your dignity, married friends!
Consider the beauty of your calling!
Consider - **your vocation** was **first**
> in the heart of God
> > and
> **so precious and good**
> **he entrusted his own son**
> **to a married couple.**
We celebrate and commemorate today the Holy Family of Bethlehem
and Nazareth,
> but
every family,
every true marriage is holy by the **very fact that it exists**, for it is
> > > the institution,
> > > the reality
> > at the foundation of God's
> > plan for the human race.

Out of the **family grew the Church**, because the Lord Jesus went from
family life with Joseph and Mary into His public life where He called
together the disciples
> and the Twelve Apostles
> and the early Church.
A product of the Holy Family formed the holy family of God which is
the Church we know and love. **Such is the dignity of the family that
it is difficult to exaggerate.** I need not tell you that everything I've said
about family is imbedded in our religious thinking. Also I need not tell
you that almost everything about the family is under attack by many who
do not share the Christian faith. The proponents of the culture of death
are not committed Christians.

You know that many say our **culture**, our civilization,
> is disintegrating because of the weakness
> of family life.
Not many see a relationship between religious culture and family life.
Here is the connection.
> > **Cult** is the root of the word **culture**.
> > **Cult** speaks of **religion** and values
> > based, in our case,
> > on the Bible and Church teaching.

Take religious teaching,
take **cult** out of **culture**, and you don't have culture.
You have chaos and disintegration.
The chaos and breakdown starts in the family and is transmitted to the
culture. Do those who want to totally privatize religion,
> keep it out of the public area altogether,
> do they know they are attacking the
> foundations on which was built
> our society with its great and special rights?
>> Free speech.
>> Trial by jury and peers.
>> Free assembly.
>> Freedom of religion.

You know what? - I am convinced many who want no religious content
> to public education
> or government,
> no display of religious symbols or words
>> in courtrooms
>> public parks or public buildings,
> are perverse enough to know exactly what they are doing, for
> these people are self-haters, as any one must be who has put full
> and total faith in human institutions and lived to see them fail
> with tragic regularity and tragic consequences.
Respect, **cult**ivate, (the word "cult" again), cultivate the religious cult-
based values of family life and you preserve **a culture**,
> a nation,
> a society,
> and of course, you preserve family.
Dear married, friends,
Dear children, young or old,
> value, cherish family life.
The Holy Family had problems, as the gospel today shows us. What
family could have a greater problem than to have their only son
murdered. But in Christ all things hold together, most especially family
life, and if **family life** holds together, then so do …individuals,
>> communities,
>> parishes,
>> nations.

Study,
Meditate on,
Pray about
 the Holy Family of Nazareth and Bethlehem.

 Notice the center of the **family** was the child
 who was also God.
 God was the center of family life -
 It was firm, stable, peaceful
What problems the Holy Family had came from outside the family,
not from the relationships **in** the family.
Determine to make God the center of your family.
 Family prayer
 Family attendance at weekly Mass
 Family times for the sacrament of penance
 Family times to talk and enjoy each other.
Make God your first priority, your family and your marriage your
priority of second importance, and worry not -
  the new year
   the new century
    will be a peaceful and happy time for
    you and your family
    and for the culture, the nation,
    the church.

Like Mary the mother in the small family of Nazareth,
  let us ponder both the natural and the supernatural
  mysteries of God in our hearts.

Guess What? God's Still Here!

In some parts of the world it is already a new year and a new century.
I confess to you today that I feel no particular emotion about Y2k.
I confess to you also that I have no particular
concern as to what man or woman is declared **person** of the century
        by whatever institution or news agency.
        or what will be declared the **greatest**
        event of the **past** hundred years
        or what the **crystal ball** predicts for the
        21st century.

It is of more interest to me to realize that what
 matters in history is not always the things that
happen,
      but also the **things that refuse to happen**.

At the beginning of this century (which has only a few hours left for us)
        many crystal ball gazers said,
        the **end** of history's religious phase
        will come in the 20th century.

Those people, now long dead (and their successors in our own day),
        refused to accept the fact that Christianity
        is built on the only **real or lasting**
        "new"- ness that has happened since the
        beginning of the world.

The only real or lasting "new"- ness happened in a
        small village
        in a tiny country.

The infinite Son of the infinite Father was born of Mary of Nazareth.
He grew up to preach an exalted doctrine
    of gentleness and
      humility,

purity of heart,
self sacrifice,
love
and redemption.
He came to share our humanity so that we might share his divinity.

It was a new message, which an old world didn't like so Jesus of
Nazareth died a **crucified failure.**

Today, our world, which likes to triumph it's
successes and professes no real need for God,
Counts it's years from the birth of the **crucified failure.**
It's the end of a century which began with
the opinion makers of the year 1899 and 1900
saying that religion would end before the
century ended!
Well, how wrong they were.

Jesus is the **new** wonder of every day and every century since
the day of his birth.

One theme in Jesus' teaching is especially thought provoking today.

It also explains why we Christians and Catholics need not fear the
challenges of the next century. The **central theme** of Jesus' teaching is
that God,
not man
or woman, is **the final authority.**

God has **rights.**
Human beings have **duties.**

We deny God **His** right to our own peril. Our century did that and it cost
us rivers of blood , bottomless pits of tears, a virtual abyss of misery.
Our crucified failure is the one Living **Lord** of history.
A Lordship which he will exercise to
the final minute of the final day of the world.

Fear not, **little flock**, our Lord has said:
"I am with you all days until the end of the world."
And we are more than just **"Little Flock"**

23

we are
> God's adopted children with the spirit
> of his Son in our hearts and so we can
> address the Lord of every century as

> "Father"

how secure,
how humble,
how obedient,
how grateful we should be
> > because the crucified failure has shared
> > His victory with us.
> > We are heirs to eternal life.
Heirs, **if** we remember God has **rights,**
> > we have **duties**
Jesus is the only genuine "new"- ness which surpasses
 all human hopes and expectations
> > and as such He remains,
> > > forever, from age to age
> > > > century to century
> > > > > millennium to millennium.

The shepherds in the gospel found something totally new.

They became missionaries immediately
They told everything they had learned and seen
> to everyone who would listen.
And they were effective missionaries.
> > > The gospel says,
> > > All who heard their story were
> > > amazed at what had been told to
> > > them by the **shepherds**

That "new"- ness of Jesus must capture our hearts and live again.
Only a rediscovered **newness of Jesus** and his message will make the
new century really new.

> Without the **newness of Jesus**
> the new century will seem very old,
> > > very quickly.
Because all the old human sins, hatreds, jealousies will be revisited.

On this feast of the **maternity of Mary,
the motherhood of Mary**

I suggest this:
    In your own heart dedicate the century to yourself and
    to Mary the mother of the Lord of history.
    She wants her son's work to be a success.
    Her son's work **is you, me, the church** and the living human soul.

Her son's work is to bring us to the Peace only He can give in eternal life.

    Beg Mary, the **Queen Mother**, to help bring this about.

Finally, I leave you with the beautiful blessing of the reading,
a most fitting blessing for a new year and a new century.

                    The Lord bless you and keep you.
                    The Lord let his face shine upon you
                    and be gracious to you.
                    The Lord look upon you kindly and
                    give you peace.

Who Did the Wise Men Find?
Truth!

Rise up in splendor, Your **light** has come,
      the glory of the Lord shines on you.

See **darkness** covers the whole earth
      but upon **you** the Lord **shines**.

Splendidly beautiful words from the master poet, Isaiah.

Your light has come, the glory of the Lord shines on you.

In our day we hear a lot about people seeking the **truth,**
        seeking meaning,
        seeking to find oneself.

In our day we hear a great deal
about the virtue of an **open mind.**
About the backwardness of accepting absolute **truth.**

We hear a great deal about being **true to ourselves.**
We hear a great deal about **creating our own truth.**

     That idea was enshrined in a Supreme Court
     decision when one of the wise men of the
     Supreme Court, U.S.A. wrote,
     "It's up to every person to determine the
     truths about life and it's meaning."
Well, now.
The gospel speaks of Wise Men seeking **the Truth** about the star.
They embarked on a two year journey.
They must have been dismissed as lunatics
       madmen
    by many when they said to other

26

travelers that they were following a
star to find a new born King.
They traveled **in darkness**---you **need** to travel in darkness
to follow star light. They were **seekers.**

Can we imagine the surprise at journey's end when they didn't find
an infant King in a **palace!**
They found an **infant** in a poor **carpenter's** home.
They found a young **mother** in a peasant's drab dress.
The **father's** hands were thickly callused.

They planned, I'm sure, to be ushered into a bright gilded hall for an
audience with the new born King. Instead they had to bend their heads
to enter the semi-darkness of a tiny house.
They did not find their **imagined notion** of how
a new born King should appear
nor find him in king like surroundings.
But why are the Wise Men remembered?
Why are they called **Wise Men**?

Because they didn't try to impose their notions
of truth on the **truth** they found.
They didn't try to create a truth more appealing to them---
they humbly accepted the **truth they found.**

They allowed their minds and wills to be
shaped and formed by the truth in front of them.

We think of the gifts they offered.
The greatest gift they offered was their mind, their faith.
They **accepted the fact before them**: The new born King was a child
a peasant's son
and he lived in very
humble surroundings

And **finally** for those of our age who take up
seeking as a way of life, who **cultivate the open mind** to the
detriment of never **settling on** anything;

To those, the Wise Men offer a jolt of reality.
The Wise Men quit their seeking…
they had **found the truth** in the new born King

and the gospel tells us,
"They **departed** for **their home country** by another way."
The search was ended, the light of Truth
                              flashed in their minds---
                              they went home
                              satisfied, fulfilled and surely pondering a
                              mystery they didn't and couldn't understand.
They couldn't get their inquiring minds around the
                              mystery of a child whose birth was announced
                              by a chorus of angels
                              and by a star.
But, they didn't **use their minds** as
                    the **measure of the things** which were
                    clearly of God's doing-even if it
                    was a God they did not know.

The Wise Men did not try to create Truth...
        They accepted it.

Who does create truth, you ask?
Answer: It's a **growth** industry **in our** country.
                    Ever hear someone say by word or action that---
                    The ten commandments are of the dark ages.
                    The sexual morality taught by the Bible and the church
                    is of the dark and dreary past.
                    The abortion issue is purely a matter of choice.
                    That one religion is good as another.
                    That marriage is good, so long, as love lasts.
                    That my conscience is my absolute guide
                    That absolute truth is a **dark** ages fantasy.

Friends the **darkness** in all those positions is in the
mind of the one who holds to or lives by such
sad positions.

Each and all are **creating** their **own truth.**
They are making their minds and their prejudice the measure of truth.
They do not bow humbly before the truth which God
has put in front of them.

We can not create truth.

We can only discover Truth that has been there all along.

The oil prospector who finds
an oil deposit did not create it.
It was there all the time. He simply found it.

If the Hubbell telescope sends back astonishing,
wondrous pictures of the universe previously
never seen, the telescope or the astronomer
didn't create the **Truth** of the
existence of those far away worlds.
                                    They only found them.

The most sophisticated electronic
wizardry is only the result of
someone discovering a Truth always
there; that these things work together
in this astonishing way.

There is no **creating** of Truth, there is only discovery
                                    of Truth.

And when discovered, the wise person
                    like the Wise Men of the gospel
                    bow before it and go
                    home carrying the precious
                    new gift of Truth in their
                    minds and hearts.

God created the Truth of the far away galaxies
                                    and the tiniest neutron and

                    The truth about human life,
                                    sin and virtue
                    The truth about marriage
                                    about sex
                                    about life and death.
We **humans only work at discovering it** and
we can also forget Truth even after it's discovered.
If we are arrogant enough to think we can create
Truth we will need to live with the consequences.

Things will disintegrate.

Christ, the new born king is **God's Truth** about **everything.**
That's why the first reading says,
darkness covers the earth
but upon you the Lord shines.

Some teachings of the Bible and the Church are beyond
the human mind to grasp but the divinely
guided teaching office of the church leads us
on like a star pointing to Christ,

and the wise man,
the wise woman

like the Wise Men of the gospel say "I believe"
I seek no longer
I have found God's revealed Truth

and those who do so go home another way

changed by the wonder
of finding the Truth
God has revealed

and observing the darkness in which so many chose
to live their lives the person of faith rejoices
in the words of Isaiah

Rise up in splendor for your light has come

the glory of the Lord shines upon you.

Baptism: Call to Holiness

Many have visited the great National Shrine
of the Immaculate Conception in Washington D.C.

The large and impressive church has been in various
stages of construction for decades.

Who knows how many millions of dollars
have been poured into that building for
the greatest purpose in all the world.

The **purpose,** when all is said and done,
is to raise up a sacred space dedicated
precisely to God's glory
and to honor the mother of Jesus.

At the heart of the nation
which is without question the
fruit of the world in terms of
military power
economic power
social power
secular power

there stands the Baptism of the Immaculate Conception

a counterpoint,
an argument against the
nation that all significant power in that city rests
on the White House
the Supreme Court
the Pentagon
Capital Hill

The shrine church of the Immaculate Conception reminds all
there is another power in our world
a power finally more

important than anything taken
terribly seriously by the
          power managers,
          power sultans,
          power brokers

In the District of Columbia

There is a power and a presence in the life of nations and the life of individuals greater and more lasting than any merely human government. There is a Lord and Master of history and nations to whom every living soul in government is finally accountable.

That great shrine of the Immaculate Conception is constantly being enriched with new treasures of art.

At the present a huge new sculpture is being
Prepared…
          It will be 50ft wide
          17ft high;

          it is being carved from very precious marble;

          it will be positioned in such a way that
          anyone leaving the Basilica will see it

and what will the viewer see?

          A marble picture of men and women of every race
                culture
                ethnic and language group
But the sculpture doesn't stop there.

          Over all, there's   **a dome**

          representing the Holy Spirit and from
          that dome rays of light go out
          touching each person individually
          with God's grace and glory.

          The sculpture will remind all
          that we are **called to holiness** from
          the day we were **baptized** and admitted

                                        into the infinite company of Father,
                                                            Son,
                                                            Holy Spirit

Called to **holiness** because of a new spirit let loose in the world

                    God's Holy Spirit

That marble picture in that church in the heart of
 the capital of our nation powerfully illustrates the
 tension between the secular power and spirit that demands
our allegiance and the Holy Spirit
of the God who has called us---

                                        set us apart as His holy portion
                                        anointed us with His Holy Spirit
                                            in baptism
                                            in confirmation with the
                                            Holy Eucharist

He has called us to be **totally** His, **committed to Him**

        He demands our **full allegiance**.

Here is the
spirit of the **world** in all it's power and temptation all around us.

        the spirit of **God** has been given us---
            what spirit will be our inspiration?

        The spirit of the world and worldly power or
        the spirit of God and Godly power,
                        humility,
                        faith,
                        self-discipline

Like the basilica raised up in the heart of the city of worldly power
of D.C....

so **we** are God's **temple** raised up for all
 to see in a world that dismisses God as no more
                                        than a private illusion.
        Our power is as nothing if we do not

rely on the power of holiness,

But if we do there is immediate
tension in our lives.

Tension between the call of the world to rely
on the spirit of the age
the call to rely on the Holy Spirit of God the Lord of every age,

tension between the call to pride, an accomplishment or the call to
humble gratitude
because God has done great
things for us

That same tension is found in today's gospel

Jesus of Nazareth-Son of Mary
A carpenter
is baptized by John--along with many other carpenters,
shepherds,
fishermen,
women and men,
shop keepers

but something happens when Jesus is baptized...

a **voice** proclaims this is My Son
a **dove** hovers to the wonder that
in this ONE, there is a new spirit
a new man
a new tension
in the world

this Jesus is the One spoken of by Isaiah

Here is My servant,
My Chosen One Whom I uphold
the One upon whom I have **put my spirit**
the One I have grasped by the hand
I have set as a light for the nations.

This Jesus is also the ONE who went home to Nazareth
and was thrown out of town when he claimed the words

of Isaiah the prophet were fulfilled in him.

I Am the **Messiah**
I Am the **Promised One**. Jesus said.

The Nazarene neighbors of Jesus did not like the **tension**
he brought into their lives

They sensed the tension between the world they could see
the world of play and work,
the world of marriage and family,
the world of business and commerce,
the world **they wanted to call the real world**
the sensible,
tangible world
and the spirit to which they
must respond if Jesus really
were the Messiah.

Our baptism was the **most important day** of our lives

It brought us into the intimate
company of the all-Holy God

It also produces the tension in which
we most necessarily live our lives

We have been, each and all, called to holiness
this is the first vocation of each of us.

If you are young or old,
married or single,
rich or poor,
consecrated religious or lay person,
healthy or sick,
doctoral degree or high school diploma,
professional person or day laborer,
man or woman...

You are called to holiness---you are called to live the tension between
the culture of life.

and the culture of death,
the culture of raw reason and
the culture of faith,

the culture of "I'll do as I wish"
and the culture of "I'll do as God
commands"

You are called to a commitment, not to be compromised by the world.

You are called to be a holy people,
                    a people set apart,
                    an heroic people,
                    God's portion visible.

        A people aware that by God's gracious mercy
we are called to share eternal life and have
that hope because of that one baptized in the
Jordan and proclaimed to be God's own son
and into whose infinite company and mission we are
called by our Baptism when the Holy Spirit of God
marked us as God's daughter, God's son.

Pat Sweeney ~
Humble Acceptance

First of all this afternoon a word of sympathy and consolation for

Dave, Darrell, Michael, Christy, Katie

Pat's parents, Robert and Bernice

aunts and uncles, other relatives

and many friends.

Allow me a purely personal note today.
The most difficult homilies to fashion for me are those for Christmas---
Easter--- Pentecost.
The mystery and the wonder is so rich, so overwhelming
it is difficult for me
to catch the light from only one facet and focus on it.
I feel somewhat the same today.

Patricia was a very special, very rich person.
And to catch the light from all the facets of this jewel of a person
is very difficult and I will not succeed.
Over the past months I have been at Pat's bedside repeatedly.
When it became evident that this dear woman was not going to be with
us long, I started writing a few things down after I left the Sweeney
home. One night Pat assured me, she had nothing to worry about
because she said:
"God is Irish, you know."

Another time,
"Dave gives me a drug before he goes to Church so I don't trash the
house when he is gone."
As Christmas came near, she said,
"Christmas to us has two main events---
Going out with the whole **family** to cut the Christmas tree
and **Midnight Mass.**"

A few days before Christmas…Saturday night before Christmas, I was there. When I returned I wrote on my yellow pad. "Pat reminds me of the Christmas Child. So small, so humble. So simple, so peaceful. So secure in the love of God and the love of Dave and the kids."

In her final illness, Pat truly lived those beautiful words of the Easter Vigil. "Death where is your victory. Death where is your sting?" Pat fairly laughed at death. Her profound faith convinced her, "On this mountain the veil which veils all people, the web of death woven over all people has been stripped away. Let us rejoice! The God to whom we looked has saved us."

This humble, simple lady --- gracious, kind, wise--- sought to find the Child of Bethlehem.

Her humble heart cried out to God to give her the grace of total commitment to Christ and to the Church.

Like the Wise Men of the Gospel, she made a diligent search for that Child
and she found the Child and His Mother.
She went to the manger repeatedly to visit with the Mother and Child as she said her daily rosary.
She begged of the Child, mercy and guidance as she said the Chaplet of Divine Mercy.
In the mysteries of the Rosary she followed the Child from birth
to death
to Resurrection.
And when she had taken on the qualities of a child in her final illness she shared, willingly in the moment when, the Child of Bethlehem grown to manhood, died
a cruel death on the Cross.
She suffered her own crucifixion.
In the spirit of the Child of Bethlehem she said,
"Father, into Your hands I give my life."

Quiet,
humble and uncomplaining
strong and simple
to the very last.

Last Saturday night, Pat prayed with us a decade of the rosary.
We meditated with her on the mystery of the Resurrection.
Her crucifixion was about over. The day of New Life was dawning.
She was a woman of almost mystical qualities.
One day she was speaking about her love for the Mass she said,
"Father, I can almost see the crowds of angels around the altar when
Mass is being celebrated."
When she said that she was saying exactly what the Book of Revelation
says about the liturgy of heaven of which the liturgy of earth
is powerful but veiled participant.

Dave, Children, Parents, Friends... you have lost to death one whose
whole soul breathed love for you.

Maybe Mother's greatest act of love for you was her manner of death.
It was slow, but so strong and faith-filled.
Only gradually did this precious gift leave you and your home.

You had months to show your tenderness, your love and your strength
of spirit---a strength which matched hers.
A mutual strength, which only hearts locked in love can ever know.

Pat lived her faith. And Pat was a teacher of the faith.
A faith which she saw so precious and good
that only a powerful urgency to share it did justice to the gift.

Her heart flowed out to her students when she talked of
Christ and the Church.
Consecrated as a Marian Catechist, she lived her consecration.
She used her talent. Fr. Scheckel moved her from teaching the
7th grade over to 3rd grade Religious Education because he wanted the
best to prepare that First Communion class.

Poor souls who had wandered from the faith of their youth were
persuaded by Pat to return to Christ and the Church.

She was the kind of woman of which our Holy Father so
often speaks. The faith - filled **lay person** who brings
Christ to the streets, the market place, the office, the home.

And she did it with such gracious joy and uplifting words that
no one could object.

She so loved the sacrament of penance - she wept over her own sins---
I know.
Her love for this moment of God's mercy flowed into the hearts of her 6th
grade students who often asked the improbable question, "When can we
go to confession again?"

But now all of this treasure is taken from us. Yet... how wondrous our
Christian faith. Death has gained only a terribly wasted body.
It has not captured the Spirit of this woman. She defied death's threat to
take from her,

> her faith,
> her love of God,
> her trust in God,
> her love of family and friends,
> her hope of eternal life.

Pat knew with the divine wisdom only faith can give what Saint Paul
said in the 2nd reading:
"Don't you know that we who were baptized were baptized into Christ's
death so that just as Christ rose from the dead to a new life so we, too,
will be raised with Him to a New Life."

In all my years of priesthood I have never felt the **power, the beauty,**
and **the joy** of giving Holy Communion to a person as I did when I gave
the Lord to Pat these past months. The words,

> "When you eat My body and drink My blood you have eternal
> life in you."

It was an enormous consolation for me – the **wonder** and the **power of
those words** as Pat would take Eternal Life into her cancer-ravaged
body and faith-filled spirit. What a joy our Catholic faith and never a
greater joy than on a day such as today.

Monday I came into Church. It was chilly and dark.
In the morning on Monday, Dave called to say Pat died.
I picked up my breviary for Evening Prayer.
The first words I read warmed and brightened the Church and my spirit.
In conclusion, I will read the hymn for

Evening

Prayer

last Monday............

40

"Now fades all earthly splendor,
The shades of night descend;
The dying of the daylight
Foretells creation's end
Though noon gives place to sunset,
Yet dark gives place to light;
The promise of tomorrow
With dawn's new hope is bright

The silver notes of morning
Will greet the rising sun,
As once the Easter glory
Shone round the Risen One.
So will the night of dying
Give place to heaven's day,
And hope of heaven's vision
Will light our pilgrim way.

So will the new creation
Rise from the old reborn
To splendor in Christ's glory
And everlasting morn.
All darkness will be ended
As faith gives place to sight
Of Father, Son and Spirit
One God, in heaven's light. "

In those words are the foundation of **our hope, our peace, our comfort, our joy...**

On this day of Pat's funeral.

Father Into Your Hands
I Commend My Suffering

Pope John Paul II has been photographed   skiing
                                                 hiking
                                                 boating
                                      as a victim of gun shot
                                      speaking to the UN
                                      visiting presidents and kings
                                      visiting prisons and palaces
                                                 praying
                                                 playing
                                                 talking
                                                 eating
          He is surely the most photographed person living or who has
ever lived.

There is a new photograph -   in my judgment
                                and only mine so far
                                      as I know . . .
                          The most moving and powerful photograph
                                      and
                    one that should be   studied
                                           and reflected on
                                           prayed over.

It's a candid shot,   no posing
                          no make up applied.

It is a perfect picture for this World Day of Prayer
                                for the sick and the suffering.

It is a picture of the pope from the back.
                    He is walking alone
                                      on a path that disappears
                                      off the photograph.

He's an old man now.
You can see the weakness
in that once powerful frame.
He is walking with a cane.
His shoulders are stooped.

It's the very picture of a sick, weak man
                walking into the
                future slowly but deliberately and with purpose.
John Paul spoke to a group of elderly and sick people recently.
                He began by saying:
                        I'm growing old with you.
                        I'm sick with you.
The days of young strength and energy are gone
                        not to return.
                        I'm growing old with you.
                        I'm growing sick with you.
John Paul, the good shepherd to his flock
                the good pastor to his people,
uses a word which he himself made famous:
                "solidarity".
He wants to be seen now not only as the supreme
head of the Church
        not only as Christ's supreme temporary substitute on earth
                as supreme teacher
                administrator and legislator for his far flung flock,
Now he wants to be seen also in full solidarity
with the weakest of his flock.
But that alone is not enough - after all many
a courageous doctor or nurse
                missionary
                        or
                humanitarian
                        has cast his or her lot
                        entirely with the weak
                                the suffering
                                the aged
They've lived their adult lives in solidarity with those
who have come to almost all the birthdays they are going to see.
Simply being present to these people is a
great gift to them

and
a great act of charity and compassion on the part of the caregiver.
But finally it is not enough.
                    There is still the great void
                        the emptiness
                                which suffering and the
                                certainty of death inspire.
This is where the suffering Pope adds a splendid
uplifting dimension.
A dimension that saves us from the
despair that sets in for those who have no hope in Christ.

This despair deeply infects our society.
            A despair which has a living and evil
            face we have seen and heard about.
                    Dr. Kevorkian of assisted suicide infamy
                    is the incarnation
                            the living, breathing
                            enfleshment of despair.
And the great sadness is that he is not alone.
At least one state, Oregon, has enough voters
so filled with despair about life that they
voted to legalize assisted suicide and euthanasia.
That is the final step for a society which values life
            only so long as it is   productive
                                        beautiful
                                        perfectly formed and functioning
                                        wanted
                                        needed
                                        useful
                                        convenient
                                        planned
and every other word in the dictionary that is
            self-centered
            faith-less
            whole-less.
                        despairing of life,
                        people use to describe as the "good life".
These words
this mind set is the perfect recipe for bitter despair,

sooner or later
because life is not accepted as a gift in all its moments

but
despair comes along, always,
when life is treated as a commodity which must be
useful for my desires and   my needs,
my pleasures.
But as every child who's ever had   a toothache
or
earache knows,
life isn't always as I want it.

What to do then?   What to do?

Pope John Paul – first, teacher of the Church
and now
first sufferer of the Church
shows the way to all by deliberately and gratefully
walking in the great light that streams
from the Cross of Christ.
For the ill,
For the aged,
the Cross of Christ is a blazing beacon of hope.

In the cross of Christ is the hope and healing
a despair-filled society needs.

"By His Cross we were healed"
the Sacred Scripture says.

Our society sees   no possible purpose in suffering,
no possible purpose in weakness
no possible purpose in illness.

That attitude
that mindset
reveals how profoundly
pagan and secular thinking has
penetrated into the inner workings of our society.

Must we try to alleviate suffering and pain??
Absolutely - after all, what everyone remembers of Christ

is that He healed   the lepers
        the blind
        the sick of every kind.
But the Divine Physician did not take Himself from the cross,
     and only the unbelieving thug on the cross next to Him,
     and some of the bystanders
     suggested it.
Suffering
Human weakness
Human pain
freely accepted was the instrument of our salvation.
God always, always turns things upside down.
     When Christ seemed, in the view of all the world
     as the weakest,
     He was the strongest.
I speak to all who know pain and weakness in their lives,
     physical, mental, emotional,
        Now may be your strongest moment.

     Study the Cross of Christ.
     Love the Cross of Christ.
        Join your sufferings
           to Christ, the first sufferer.
See there the meaning of your suffering.
See there the mode and manner in which to defeat
     meaningless in your suffering
     despair in your soul and spirit.
See in the Cross
See in your suffering a moment flooded with hope
     because Christ the Divine Healer
        Christ the Divine sufferer
           rose from the dead
           to a totally new life.

     He has taken hold of suffering
        and stripped it of despair
        made it the very key to a new life.
Our Holy Father
     walking away from the camera,
        stooped shoulder,
        cane,

short, unsteady steps
walking in a path which goes beyond the camera's range
beyond this life
accompanied by his suffering he is walking
calmly
faithfully
hopefully
into eternal life.
Christ is our divine teacher whose great lesson for life
Is the Cross.
John Paul is our Christ's substitute, temporary teacher
of all the wondrous things he's written
none are so powerful
as the lesson he teaches with his suffering
and the sickness willingly accepted
in solidarity with the suffering Christ, who said

Father, into Your hands I give My life.

The Rules Don't Change

On this July morning the liturgy puts before you and me
        difficult words from the Bible.
The words are not difficult to understand.
On the contrary,
        the texts are difficult because they are easy to understand.
In the first reading God complains that His people are a sinful
                                obstinate
                                rebellious lot.

And He tells the prophet Ezekiel,
        "Say to them: 'Thus says the Lord God.'"
God goes on to warn the prophet Ezekiel:
        If you do not warn the people about their sins
        and they go on sinning -
        they will die because of their sins,
        but so will you for not warning them as I sent you to do.
It is the preacher's job in every generation
        to warn the people
        and it is no fun
After all, even Jesus was run out of his home town for doing that
        and finally hung on a cross for proclaiming that He was the truth
        about God,
                man and human life.
Ezekiel had an advantage in his day, long ago.
People were willing to **admit to sinfulness**
        but they were not prepared to give up their ways
        not prepared to repent
        not prepared to be converted.
In our day people are not willing to **admit they have sinned**
        and so the words of the prophet fall not on deaf ears
        but on ears and souls conditioned to wonder
                "What is that man talking about?"
                "Who is that man talking about?"
                "Where did he get his wisdom?"

In a serious way our world has done what Christ Himself could not do -
       it has overcome sin.
Sin has been overcome by the simple, expedient rewriting of the rules.
In the past century every Christian church of whatever name
       preached God's condemnation of   birth control
                         and
                         abortion
       Almost every state in the union had laws put in place by
       non-Catholic legislators
       against the sale of contraceptive devices.
       But, you say, the people wanted the rules changed.
In the days of Ezekiel, people were doing as they pleased,
       rewriting the laws of God to their own preferences.
And God said to Ezekiel: "GO TO THEM
         and say,
         Thus says the Lord God . . ."
Weak and selfish humans have rewritten the rules
       about fornication which we now call safe sex
       about homosexual marriages as in Vermont
       and a few church bodies
       about abortion.
As it has in the minds of five Supreme Court justices and millions of our
people:
       has it ever occurred to you
       that we have a heavy concentration of adolescent thinking on the
Supreme Court of our land?
       Adolescents, God bless them, like fun and pleasure
         without responsibility.
       The Supreme Court folks tell us
         that mind-set is perfectly acceptable.
       Or that sterilization surgeries are an epidemic in our country -
         the great sins of yesteryear have become
         the rewritten rules of our day
         to accommodate a mentality that is, in practice
           Atheism,
           and Paganism
           revisited.
God, in His Fatherly, loving care and wisdom
       did not allow something so precious as the truth to be left to a
majority vote of people who live by and for their own happiness now,
without a thought of the next life to come.

He said:
    "I am the Lord your God
        and I put before you this wise and good law."
Rules and laws by which to live our life
    and how tragic and strange things become
    when we forget those laws.
Strange and tragic: For instance
            Now we have the horror of infanticide in our country
            legally established by five justices of the Supreme Court.
        At the same time, these are some who have mounted
        a great effort to rescue penguins from an island
        soaked in oil somewhere in a vast ocean.
            We also have a group of people
            putting together a ship to sail that same ocean
            to provide abortion possibilities
            where otherwise that procedure might not be possible.

        How strange and tragic
                save birds
                kill babies
It is the prophet's job,
        the Sacred Scripture tells us today,
        to warn people of their sins.

And to constantly remind the people of the goodness
                                        the wisdom
                                        the justice
                                            of God's Law

We need more authentic prophets in our day
        and if we get them we are blessed.
        And if we listen to them we are twice blessed.
The saddest lament in the Old Testament is the comment:
        "The voice of the prophet was not heard in the land
                and
        everyone did as they pleased."

Mary
A Mother's Model

It is an honor to be with you this morning.
For those who are not members of Blessed Sacrament Parish –
I welcome you.
To the committee of women who organized this special day,
  I extend to you my appreciation and gratitude
    and the appreciation and gratitude of all gathered here.

It was not by accident, I'm sure,
that you chose the commemoration of the Blessed Mother's birthday
  to bring together mothers
  for the purpose of praying for your own children
  and children generally.
    And to extend your mother's hearts
    to the children of Cameroon
    with an offering of money to help those poor kids.
When I look at you this morning I recognize
  I am looking at the real power in the Church
            in the community
            in our homes and
              schools
I hope you recognize, Mothers, that there is no power in all the world
  that can match the power of knees bent humbly
 in prayer before God
  and a heart attached to the font of infinite mercy.
A Mother's celebration in the sight of the Crucifix
  which was the moment of supreme sorrow
  for the Mother of the Crucified who stood beneath the Cross.
Mary followed her Son's life cycle from conception to death.

In the liturgy of the Church,
  Mary's birthday today is followed one **week** from **today**
  with the commemoration of **Our Lady of Sorrows.**

51

Spliced in between these two
is the commemoration of **The Triumph of the Holy Cross!**
Mary, the mother, followed her child from conception to death.
> She accepted the pains of His birth into life as a newborn.
> She accepted the pains of His birth into a new life
>> beyond the Cross.
And from conception to Calvary, Mary was **puzzled**
> at both the wonder
>> and
> the horror which entered her life
> and her Son's life.
She marveled at the angels who announced His birth.
She felt deep in her mother's heart
the mockery and humiliations heaped upon her Son and herself at His death.

And what did Mary do with the puzzles which were
> her child, her Son and His life?
>> **She contemplated these things in her heart.**
That is simply to say she **prayed** about these things.
> She prayed for her Son
>> the safety and success of His life.
She prayed for wisdom and patience for herself.
She prayed for Him at birth and at death.
She prayed for her family.

> **She prayed** . . . and mothers, think on this . . .

Mary taught her son all the purely human virtues.
> To pray is a human virtue.

Jesus was truly Mary's Son.
> Now, how easy it is to recognize a mother's handiwork
>> in her sons and daughters?
In the Bible we never have an explicit word
> that says Mary prayed.
> But her **Son** is praying constantly.
> You wonder how he got all the other things done.

He even ran away from the crowds
> who thought they needed Him
>> **to pray**.

Of this constant praying of Jesus, one truly can say
        "Like mother, like Son."
Mothers, you want you children to pray?
Let them see you as a woman of prayer.
Hold your children to your heart in prayer.
Mothers, it is sad but true -
        motherhood is under attack in our day.
It is a sign of the perversion of so much that once was good in our
society
        that the font of life
        the heart of the home
        the fullness of womanhood
        the flower of humanity
        Motherhood
        is under attack from so many quarters.

And your children are under attack as well.
Oh, it doesn't seem like attack
        only because we have become accustomed to it, but
                every waking moment, your child,
                young or old,
                is the object of someone trying to **sell something**
                        to him, to her, to them.
        Your child
        your children
        have been reduced to something less than
                the beautiful
                precious
                        human person
                                God gave you.
                Your child in our society
                has become mainly an economic unit.
Your child is being used, continually,
        as a source of economic profit
        and the politicians keep telling us that the economy must be
kept booming, which, in translation, means that more and more, you
and I
but, especially, your children, who don't know what's happening to
them
will be seen less and less as persons and
 more and more as economic units.

53

It's the new slaughter of the **innocence** of the **innocents.**
And they don't know what's happening to them
        as the velvet gloves of consumerism
        gently push them in the direction of seeing themselves primarily
        as happy, content consumers.

But so many kids are not happy and not content.
Their precious souls and spirits need so much more
        than the latest in   athletic shoes
                                     computer games
                                       electronic gadgets
        or, Lord help us,
                                     safe sex.

Your kids need Jesus.
What are you Mothers to do?

      "In the pale light of the late afternoon, the dirt road to Bullhead, S.D., on the Standing Rock Reservation, begins to fade into the rolling plans. The paved road ended 20 minutes ago and is mostly mud, known as "gumbo" to the locals because of the sticky, slippery dirt that will end in your car skidding or stuck far from home.
      Over a small rise, the town of Bullhead (pop 414) sits almost concealed in the valley below. On a small rise outside of town is the home of Germaine Eagle. In her small living room she stands and prays before two yellow candles. There is a sadness in her prayers and throughout the small communities on Standing Rock. In the past year, eight resident children have committed suicide.
      "We need really to pray for our children," says Germaine. "We have to get together and start praying for them. Because, if we don't, we're going to lose our children."

It is Jesus your children want and they may not even know it.
And it is your prayers that will bring them
        the gift of Jesus and His Holy Spirit.
Our kids are restless and even self destructive because
        a steady diet of material things clogs the veins and arteries
        of the soul which was made for God
        and will not be at peace until it finds its rest in God.
Consider the words of Pope John Paul to the 2,000,000 kids
        who went to World Youth Day in Rome:

"In fact it is Jesus you seek when you **dream of happiness**. He is waiting for you when nothing else you find satisfies you. **He** is the **beauty** to which you are so attracted. It is He who provokes you with that **thirst for fullness that will not let you settle for compromise.** It is He who urges you to **shed the mask of a false life**. It is He who **reads in your hearts** your most **genuine** choices, the **choices** that others **try to stifle**. It is **Jesus** who stirs in you the desire to do something **great** with your lives, the will to follow an ideal, the refusal to allow yourselves to be ground down by mediocrity, the courage to commit yourselves humbly and patiently to improving yourselves and society, making the world more human and more fraternal."

My dear mothers -　　　pray
　　　　　　　　　　　pray
　　　　　　　　　　　pray for yourselves and your children.

An hour a week.
Ten minutes a day on your knees before the Blessed Sacrament
　　　　　is you, Mother,
　　　　　at your most beautiful
　　　　　most powerful moment.

Finally, I have not mentioned the Cameroons or the heroic women religious who bring God's presence and face of the Good Shepherd
　　　　　to so many of God's little poor ones.
I offer you again the beautiful example of Mary,
　　　　　Mother of God.
Remember how, when she learned of her cousin Elizabeth's pregnancy,
　　　　　six months in progress,
　　　　　Mary hurried off to the hill country,
　　　　　the Scripture says.
Mary brought to her cousin the Good News of her human love
　　　　　for her older relative.
　　　　　　　　　　The good news of　　　caring
　　　　　　　　　　　　　　　　　　　　helping
　　　　　　　　　　　　　　　　　　　　concerned love
The good news of her **simple presence** during the last difficult weeks and days of pregnancy.
Her presence to help with the newborn so the exhausted mother
　　　　　　　　　　　　　　　could rest.
Mary also brought the Good News of **salvation**
　　　　　which she carried under her heart in her own developing baby.

Mary brought to her cousin Elizabeth
help for **body and soul**.
Mary is certainly the image of the perfect missionary -
one who brings salvation for the whole person, body and soul.
A great birthday present to Mary,
model of prayers
model of missionaries,
would be some goodly money gifts
so that others might go to those who need help for body and for soul.

Finally, mothers, let us be true children of Mary.
At the wedding of Cana
Mary instructed the servants to,
"Do whatever He tells you",
as she pointed to her Son.

And what has Jesus told us to do when we want to remember Him?
At the Last Supper, after changing bread and wine
into His Body and Blood, Jesus said:

"Do this in memory of Me".

This is a precious and powerful hour.
Obedient to Mary's command,
we are her true **children**.

Obedient to Christ's command
we are His true **disciples.**
Gather together all the power of this moment
and beg God's mercy on yourself
your children
and your spouse.

and on those heroes who take the mercy and message of Jesus
to the poor of the world.

Peter Murray Funeral~
My Soul Thirsts

First of all this morning--- I extend my most sincere sympathy to---
the family of **Peter.**
On my own behalf and on behalf of Blessed Sacrament Parish.

Our sympathy goes out to you Phil Jr., Jennifer, Patrick...
                    You had a brother and you called him **Peter**.

Our sympathy to relatives and friends...
                    You had an uncle, a grandson, a friend, and you
                    called him **Peter.**
Most especially our sympathy to mother and dad... Sheila and Phil

You had a son, conceived in love and nurtured in joy and you
                    called him **Peter.**
                                        and
Peter's life was rich and full   and   tragically short.

Water washed Peter's life from birth to death.
A **gushing of water** signaled the time of his birth had come.
                         The lusty crying of the new born
                         signaled both a **healthy** bundle
                         of unknown promises
                                        and
                         The **crying** of family and friends
                         at his too early funeral.

On February 10, 1974, Phil and Sheila carried this new-born
to this Church.
The **gush of water** in the moment of Baptism signaled his new birth
into Divine Life - forever an adopted son of God.
One of those of whom Christ said, "I will not lose even one of them."

You gave him a **strong** Christian name—

You called him "**Peter**".
Peter proved **true** to his strong name.
Strong in intelligence - valedictorian of his class of '92 at
Aquinas; bachelor of science in Mechanical Engineering at the
University of Minnesota 1997; engineering supervisor for
Donaldson of Bloomington, Minnesota.
His pursuit of an MBA ended by death.

Strong in body –
an athlete and a mountaineer
Peter - the name means "rock"

And

Peter was **rock** solid… in loyalty to his friends.
Rock solid… in devotion to his family.

A keen mind far beyond the ordinary… a mind focused, alert, intense
and passionate about many things…about sports,

about music,
about being
the best possible engineer,
about beauty and truth,
about the noble and the good,
wherever he could discover it.
Whether it be in a philosophy book, a history book,
a well kept garden,
a family holiday gathering
or the loyalty and devotion of a dog.
In the grand sweep of mountains and meadows,
streams and oceans.
Peter's searching mind sought the ultimate answer,
the final thrill of discovery,
the break through insight-
which cut through many questions to the single unifying answer.
In Peter's thirst to drink in the beauty
the power,
the grandeur
the mystery of nature…
he was reading and loving the first book of Revelation.
The star studded sky above,

> the tundra below,
> the sweep of a mountain valley,
> the ancient ice of a glacier,
> the icy stream,
> the majesty of the ocean,

all are but strong brush strokes of the Divine Artist who put this
lovely planet in place as our home and our gift.

Peter sought to always know more of people and of nature
and even as his knowledge of both grew---
he continued to search, to explore,
looking for the ultimate **thrill**, the ultimate **view**,
the ultimate **adventure**, the ultimate **moment** of awe and wonder.

Peter's life and his enthusiasm for life is summed up in the words
we've used several times.
> "My soul thirsts for the living God.
> When will I see Him face to face? "

In Peter's thirst to take in nature's beauty and grandeur
he drank deeply of the Divine Artist's **work.**
> Now we pray he sees the **Artist** face to face.

His restless, adventurous spirit will be at peace in that vision
because our souls were made for God and will not rest--- until they rest
in Him.

Peter's life began in a **gush** of water which brought
the **promise of life** yet to unfold.

Peter was born anew in a **gush of baptismal** water
which brought the promise of eternal life yet to unfold.

Peter's life ended
in the **overpowering gush** of waters of a glacier fed stream.

> Was Jesus asleep in the boat of life
> when the waters threatened
> and took Peter's life?

> "Master, does it not matter to
> You that I am going to drown?"

"Master does it not matter to You that our Peter
is being taken from us?"
"Master does it not matter that this brilliant,
energetic,
loving,
young man is being swept away?"
"Master does it not matter to You that this
tragic waste is unfolding before your eyes?"

"Master why do You sleep?"

"Where are You in all this water and storm?"

And Jesus said, "Peter, I was present in the water of your birth.
Peter, I was present in the water of your re-birth
in baptism.
Peter, I am present in the icy, glacial stream
because My love is constant and **sure**
as the rock which became your final resting place
in that gushing water.

Peter, I am Lord of life and Lord of death.
Peter, do not be afraid.
Peter, I am present in the waters of the tears

of your mother and dad---
in the tears
of your brothers, Phil and Pat

and sister, Jennifer

and all your friends.

Peter, in them **I weep** for you.
Their great love for you is a pale reflection
of My love for you.

But now, Peter, step out of the boat of life, walk on the water
and
Come to Me. I'm in the water
with you

and
for you
and

Do not be afraid.

What you have seen of My power and love
in the beauty of nature is nothing!
Come, Peter, I will show you the mystery of
Infinite Love behind all the wonders of nature
you loved so well.
In loving and remembering them
you loved and revered
the One who fashioned them.

Be not afraid Peter, you are about to see
the Person behind all the beauty of nature."

And can we wonder, did Peter say? : "My soul thirsts for the living God.
Now I will see Him face to face."

On this sad morning our faith, our hope, our love
impels us to accept that Peter knows that ultimate, totally, fulfilling
vision, that sweep of eternity
that luminous beauty which is eternal life.

And **that** finally **is** our peace, our consolation, our comfort,
on the day of funeral for Peter James Murray.

Who Do You Say I Am?

"Who do people say I am?"
 Who do people say I am?"

That was a very important question Jesus posed at the old resort city,
which Phillip, a small time governor of Palestine had named after the
great Caesar, far away in Rome.

The small time governor, Phillip was a big time <u>politician,</u> trying to gain
points with the super boss back in Rome.
He named a town after Caesar.
Caesaria - then he hooked his name onto it - Phillipi.

"Who do people say I am?"

Notice the answer. "The people say, you are John the Baptist,
                                        Elijah, one of the prophets."
What is important about their answers?

                    They are the wrong answers.

The <u>people</u> had it <u>wrong.</u> And what is significant about the right answer?
And there is a correct answer.

And beyond that fact someone had the right answer.

            It's very important <u>who</u> had the right answer.
                        Peter said to him

                        "You are the Christ" More full in other Gospels
Peter's answer is

                    "You are the Messiah,
                    the Son of the Living God."

Peter, the first pope had the answer and it was then
that Jesus said,

>"Thou art Peter and upon you I
>will build my church and the jaws of death shall
>not prevail against it."

>"I entrust to you the keys of the kingdom of heaven.

>Whatever you declare bound on earth will be
>bound in heaven.
>Whatever you declare loosed on earth will be loosed
>in heaven. "

This is a most important moment in God's dealing
with the human family.

**Jesus, Son of God, Savior and Lord
appointed His substitute.**

After Jesus died Peter and Peter's successors, the Bishop of
Rome, the man we call pope would
act as Christ's substitute on earth by **Christ's choice.**

>**In matters of faith and morals to hear
>Peter speak or to hear
>Pope John Paul speak is to hear
>Christ speak.**

With that background I bring to your attention a document which
Pope John Paul released to the world on August 15 of this year.

The document is entitled "The Lord Jesus."

It is a powerful **new** document but it states some
old truths of our faith

>It states there is a single church instituted by Jesus, the

Catholic Church, governed by the successor of Peter.
It states bluntly there is **no truth** in the statement **"one religion
is as good as another."**

Equality in ecumenical dialogue and action refers to the equal
dignity of the persons of various religions but **not** to **equal
sharing** in the teachings of Christ.

> Some people see Christ and the Church He founded as
> one way among many by which the full truth of God's
> revelation came to us.
> This is contrary to our Catholic faith.

> "Who do you say I am?"

The answers gleaned from the people were the **wrong** answers.
Peter, the one put in charge of safeguarding the true faith, said this about
Jesus.

> "You are the Messiah
>   You are the Son of the Living God."

Some kinds of statements are considered too blunt and too demanding
in our atmosphere of relativism, in a
pro-choice atmosphere.
Here is one of those statements taken from
the Vatican II Council.

"There exists a single Church of Christ which
subsists in the Catholic Church, governed by the
successor of Peter and by the bishops in union
with him."

Some will say "Oh don't burden us with that
hard, prickly stuff.
            Give us something of the love
and compassion of Christ.
                Don't erect barriers and walls,
                don't be segregating,
                            rather be integrating.
                Don't be exclusive, be **inclusive."**

Friends, there is no greater charity and compassion than to speak the
truth.

I ask you, is it charity or compassion for a doctor who has
discovered cancer in an unsuspecting
patient to tell that patient he/she has a
touch of the flu?

Charity for that doctor demands he
tell the patient the truth and
prescribe the hard medicine to
counteract the cancer.

Is it charity and compassion for a teacher to tell a failing
student that he/she is doing well.

Rather is not charity and compassion found in
telling the failing student the truth of his/her
academic condition.

Now, if to tell the truth about a physical or academic
condition such as passing on truth about
temporary things is important,
how much greater is the demand in charity to speak the
truth about matters which have eternal significance!

The headlines in the Times Review read
"Catholic Christianity is necessary for salvation."

is that the hard stuff which segregates
builds walls
judges
or the **charity** which flows from the sight of a
crucified Savior who went to the cross
proclaiming:
"I am the Truth
I am the Messiah
I am **the way** to eternal life, I am
the door to eternal life,
I am the Good Shepherd."

65

"Who do you say I am?"

Christ is not many but one.
Christ is not one of many ways to salvation but the one and only.
Each generation is faced with the question
put to the Apostles,

"Who do you say I am?"

Our ancient faith is a precious gift.

Our ancient faith is ultimate charity because it is
ultimate and final Truth.

That Truth is a person - his life and words are our
salvation and the only hope of eternal life.
Everything hinges on our answer to Christ's question,

"Who do you say I am?"

There Must Be The Cross

Somewhere in California is a great structure called <u>Crystal Cathedral.</u>

The ever smiling minister of that church
is famous for putting a positive spin on everything.

When that church was being built some of
his committee said there should be <u>no cross.</u>

The positive thinking minister
<u>absolutely refused</u> to entertain that
thought - he said there <u>must be a</u> <u>cross.</u>
      The cross is after all the
      central symbol of
      Christianity.
            But - he said -
            we will have a
            <u>happy</u> cross.

We must have a happy cross.

          The cross is <u>off-putting</u> and we must not have off-
putting things in a society which considers happiness
          as almost a divine right.
                    But, like cancer
                          MS
                          heart disease
                          divorce

Some things are off-putting and they are the cross as it visits our life.

Some moments of life are the despair of happy spinners unless
we remember the words we will soon use "Behold the wood
of the cross on which hung the salvation of the world."

Remembering these words allows for a happy spin to every
moment of life.
Because, because Good Friday reminds us that the
worst thing that could possibly happen has happened.
Nothing worse could be conjured up in the imagination
nor nothing worse gathered from
all the accumulated massacres,

genocide's,

disasters,

plagues and wars
of history.

Today is the day the world went
totally crazy for a few hours
and
total craziness won the day.

The puny hands of the creature spiked to a cross the hands and
heart from which has come
all the goodness
all the beauty all
the hope all the
love

the world
has known in the past knows in
the present
and
will know in the future.

This moment on Calvary is the triumph of the total madness
total craziness

of pride
of arrogance
of sin darkened minds
and souls which cannot discern
truth from falsehood
light from darkness
life from death.
But, the cross…   the cross of Christ allows us to put a happy spin on
this most insane of all moments.

Because the worst possible thing that could happen has happened

and it has been overcome. The world survived this moment
                              and been made better for it.

The cross is the instrument of victory and
the cross allows us to put a positive spin on death
                    and
                        on every diminishing moment we
                        can experience
                              whether cancer,
                                      job loss,
                                      heart disease,
                                      divorce,
                                      death of family member
Christ took those moments to the cross
as his very own and forced death to yield to life.

There is a positive spin possible for every sadness of life
because the worst sadness of all -   Christ's death
                                      on the cross did
                                      not end with death
                                      but with life.

But, don't run away from the cross to Easter - not yet.

                        We must find meaning in
                        the cross because ,most of our
                        life holds
                              small or large bits
                              of our personal
                              Calvary each day.

Stay with the cross today.
Stay with the Crucified One in mind and spirit today.
Draw meaning today, draw strength today from the cross for all
the days when you are on Calvary.

Have we ever thought our very best
        effort at raising a family

effort at marriage our very
best effort
to be a good student
our very best effort
to live a virtuous life,
a generous life has come to nothing.

Have you ever thrown your whole heart,
soul, money,
present energy and future hopes
into a project and had almost
nothing to show for it.

Cling to the cross today.

Look, listen, think.
The cross was the <u>crowning moment</u> of
the life of Jesus.
Jesus went back to the Father through the
only door <u>which would admit</u> Him.
The door marked suffering and death.

Before He dies on the cross, Jesus looks out at what He has
accomplished in His 33 years.

All His disciples are gone –
Jesus has not held their loyalty –
Jesus life is a <u>failure.</u>

At the foot of the cross is a
heart broken mother and an equally
heart broken John
On the cross Jesus saw Himself as a loser
and a <u>breaker</u> of <u>hearts.</u>

It looks as though the suffering servant of God has nothing
to show for His suffering.
<u>What trophy can the Son show the Father</u> <u>for a life spent on earth?</u>
At His side is a convicted criminal, the bottom rung of humanity,
the sub-basement of society.

This convicted criminal is the last person to speak to Jesus
before he dies.

This fellow who lived his murderous, thieving life under the cover
of darkness because he was doing the <u>works of darkness.</u>
This reprobate, now turns toward the **<u>Light!</u>**
<u>"Jesus, remember me when you come into your kingdom."</u>

Jesus turns and says to him,
>   "Truly I say to you, today you will be
>   with Me in paradise."

Jesus has his trophy to present to the Father for his life's work.
The soul of a convicted thief. That's all!

Your life seems to issue so little exciting gains or victories.

>   Cling to the Cross!

See the meaning of Jesus' life having so little to show at its end.

Your life seems to be filled with too much of sadness and defeat.
>   Cling to the Cross
Jesus returned to the Father with one poor sinner as His trophy
and yet the Father was totally pleased with the life and death of Jesus.

Let us not hurry to Easter just yet....

>   Stay at the foot of the cross
>   Learn from it.

>   There, we will learn the act of
>   putting a happy spin on the
>   Calvary moments of our life.

40th Anniversary
I Will Go To The Altar Of God

About 3 weeks ago I left a Ladies Council meeting when, in the agenda, they had come to...

"Fr. Hundt's Anniversary Party".

The last words I heard as I left the room were

"Forty Years is a long time."

Which prompts me to use the cliché.
"Today it certainly doesn't seem like a long time."

But as I gaze out here and see friends from the
Wausau days, from St. Mary's Bangor,
St. Mary's Coon Valley, St. Joseph's,
St. Peter's,
Blessed Sacrament

When I look at my dear parents,
my brothers and sisters, my uncles and aunts
cousins of many degrees,
friends from far and near...

I remember a day when we were all much younger –
Dear sister, Kathy wasn't even born - she truly was much younger!
The day of my ordination exactly 40 years ago today
                                          and the
first Mass in St. Peter's at Middle Ridge,
what splendid days they were.

I remember only a few words which I spoke back then.
I remember saying that two angels
had supported me through the seminary days and that those two angels
were sitting one on either side of me.

And here we are 40 years later and those two, Mother and Dad,
are still supporting me.

I am blessed.

Mother and Dad:
Your 66 years of marriage have taught me much about the
once and for all commitment I made as a priest.

And brothers and sisters, all ten of you...
You have been such great comfort and support, as
have the beautiful people you brought into the family through marriage,
your life partners, your children - and what a joy it is
that not one of you
has experienced the soul-ripping sadness of divorce.

My uncles and aunts, too many
to be enumerated but,
I mention my Godparents, Uncle Pete and Aunt Bernice,
Marriage is a life-long love affair.

I have been privileged to have a life long love affair with the most
beautiful Bride one can imagine.

"I saw a new Jerusalem, the Holy City, coming down out of heaven from
God, beautiful as a bride prepared for her husband,"

"I heard a loud voice from heaven crying out--- This is God's dwelling
place among men."

I see the priesthood as a gift and my life as a marriage
truly fashioned in heaven,
something truly, not fully of this earth or fashioned in the
minds of mere humans

The priesthood is a gift from God.
The Church is gift from God.
My life has been a melding of two Divine Gifts.

The Church is pictured as the bride of Christ in Sacred Scripture. When the priest acts in the person of Christ at the altar the Church becomes the bride of the priest.

My bride, the Church, has given me the proudest title a man can have the title
                    "Father".

My bride, the Church, has allowed me to bring new life into the world almost every day for 40 years.

Every man wants to see something he has created.
Most men have that joy when they see their child.
A priest knows that joy when he holds the Eucharist.
                    Here is a life
                    he has pro-created,
                    brought into existence
                    with God's help.

And that is why I have found special joy and comfort
in prayer before the Blessed Sacrament.

My bride, the Church has allowed me to bring new life
into the world and it's a comfort and a joy
               just to sit and contemplate that life,
               as a father finds joy in watching his child
               sleep or play or work.

It is a wonder to recognize that life which the priesthood allows me to bring into the world is much greater than myself.

If the father of a human child
gains some shadow of immortality
by the on-going life of his children and grandchildren…

Well, the priest brings immortality itself into the world in the person of Christ -
               the priest's work truly is forever.

Of all the radical things one might do in life,
     none is so radical
               as the priesthood.

But radical choice for me didn't mean the risky or uncertain.
It meant building the house of my life into the walls
which have the 12 Apostles as the foundation stones.

And it was not a dark adventure... for the glory of God
gave it LIGHT.
                    It's lamp was
                              Christ the Lamb.

You and I have lived through a period of history in the Church
and in society where many have lost a sense of identity,
                              lost their way.
I have retained my identity as a priest by standing at the altar almost
every day.
The altar of sacrifice,
        the altar which holds the broken body of Jesus.

When the priesthood has been a true challenge, I try to remember the
broken body of the Savior given freely for us
                              and for our salvation.

I share in the priesthood of One who was Himself the Victim.
And by His freely offered broken-ness, He saved the world.
That means I can expect to feel broken and bruised, desolate and
abandoned on occasion. It's part of the life as it is part of the bargain for
all baptized into the death of Christ.
There are days,
                    days such as today.

When one feels unworthy of the attention one gets because, one is aware
of one's inadequacy for such a gift
                    and such a privilege,
                              such a responsibility.
Then one tries to remember the miracle Jesus performed
with a couple of loaves and a couple of fish -

He took what little the small boy had to offer and fed thousands.
One day about 56 years ago the Lord asked a small 8th grade boy to give
what he had.
The young boy said "OK".   And so, here we are today.

We give willingly to Christ what little we have and allow Him to work
His wonders and feed the thousands upon thousands who come looking
for the Word and the Bread of immortality.

Today, I want to express my gratitude to all who
have provided support.
                kindness, friendship, love
                              these past 40 years.

My gratitude goes out to the good people of Blessed Sacrament who
have arranged this celebration.
I most especially at this Mass, thank God for preserving me in the
call He gave me in definitive fashion 40 years ago this weekend.

With that I finish with words which began the first Mass
I celebrated 40 years ago.
In the days when all of us were much younger,
Mass was celebrated in Latin.
Many of you will remember the beginning words well:
                  "Introibo ad altare Dei
                  Ad Deum qui laetificat juventutem meum"
In English:

"I will go to the altar of God.
To God, who gives joy to my youth."

Funeral of John Uehling, Jr.

First of all this morning a word
of most sincere sympathy on my
own behalf and on behalf of Blessed Sacrament Parish
to John and Kathy,
to the grandparents,
to all the aunts and uncles,
to all the cousins,
        to all relatives and friends.

A wonderful form of children's story is the fairy tale.

Every fairy tale begins "Once upon a time"... and
ends with, "and they lived happily ever after."

No matter how many perilous situations or evil
characters that appear in the middle of the tale,
The BEGINNING and the END are times full of hope,
joy and triumph.

Well, once upon a time a little boy was born of the love
and courage of

        John and Kathy.

It was a day filled with joy and hope and triumph,
        the little boy was cherished,
                he was the apple of the eye of his parents.

                Life was good and rich, his good parents had a son
who was healthy and bright.

The little boy was taken one splendid day to the church.
He was baptized.
He was named John, a strong, Christian, distinguished name.
                    Now the little boy was not only the son of
                    John and Kathy,
now he was also the adopted son of God.

Now he had not only the promise of a life on earth, but also
now he had the promise of everlasting life
        in heaven.
                    The little boy grew and flourished.

        He began to creep,
        he began to pull things from low tables and cabinets,
        he began to walk and talk,
        he began to ride his little bicycle,
        he patrolled the friendly neighborhood
                filled with people who had strange sounding titles like
                uncle,
                aunt,
                cousin.
                        The little boy was a friendly fellow -
                        he waved as Grandpa came by in his truck..

One day in May when the crab trees were blooming,
the maple and oaks spreading their leaves,
the robins building their nests,
the calves and lambs of spring staying close to their mothers.

On such a day our little boy came to Mother
with a slight fever.

She picked up her little boy and he nestled in her arms
and she rocked little Johnny until he fell asleep

                in the arms of mother's love.

Our little boy was put to bed, blessed with
        mother's prayer,

mother's love and with
mother's certain hope that her boy would
      be bright,
      energetic,
      and hungry
         when a spring morning's light
came across Potato Ridge Road.

But before the dawn of May 10th little Johnny slipped
silently out of the house,
    while Mother was sleeping.
    while Dad was working.

He slipped silently as a moon beam, away from
    Mother,
    Dad and brother,
    grandparents,
    uncles, aunts, cousins, and neighbors and friends.

But he did not slip away alone.

He slipped as silently as a baby's breath into
                    the arms of the One who said,

    "Let the little children come to me,
    for of such is the Kingdom of Heaven."

When Mother spoke of her baby's silent and
unexpected slipping away, she said,

    "He forever will be a good little boy."

Mother also said:
    "God gave him to us for two years
    and now He has taken him back."

I remind you every fairy tale has a happy ending...

"and they lived happily ever after."

John and Kathy,
grandparents,
uncles and aunts,
cousins and friends-

Do you see that this little boy's life is a fairy tale?

You provided a happy beginning and 24 happy months---
an evil character called death slipped into the story but...

Our Christian Catholic faith, such a joy and blessing at a time
such as this, ensures the happy ending...

He lives happily ever after -
forever a good little boy.

John and Kathy and extended family, I know that however
it is phrased, the fairy tale ending is in heaven,

the pain lingers on earth.

In your pain, turn to the Queen of May,
Mary, the Mother of God.

Like you she lost her first born Son in tragic circumstances.

Her two year old Son was threatened with death by one
of the evil characters who slipped into the life of her Son.
Mary's two year old boy escaped death - for a time.

Mary was there when total tragedy did strike her boy,
when Jesus died a crucified criminal's death.

Mary was also there for the fairy tale ending,

when her Son rose from the dead and ascended into
heaven.

And the fairy tale ending is NOT a fairy tale,
it IS God's own revealed TRUTH,
and that TRUTH spills over
into your Johnny's story, for Christ said
He was going to heaven to prepare a place for us,
and your son knows Christ's handiwork now.

Your little John will never be an angel,
but a human person in total perfection--
forever perfectly happy
forever a good little boy
and
forever grateful to Mother and Dad
for supplying the happy BEGINNING
of the fairy tale life of John Skemp Uehling, Jr.

I Am A Catholic Priest

I extend my congratulations to a new brother in the priesthood.

I am privileged and humbled to be chosen to be part of this most special
day in your life, Father O'Hara.
I congratulate you on behalf of the priests of our diocese,
                            now your special brothers and sharers
                            in Christ's priesthood.
I congratulate your dad, your family and friends, and all the people of
        Saint Ansgar's.

Most of you know the soul-stirring story of
Maximilian Kolbe.
I trust that you never tire of hearing it.   .

Recall that fateful day at the Auschwitz death camp.
The Nazi prison guards chose randomly ten men for execution
because one man had escaped.
Remember how one man chosen for the firing squad cried out
to be spared death for the sake of his family.
Picture the utter stillness when Father Kolbe spoke up,
            "I wish to take that man's place."
Imagine the sneer of the Kommandant when he asked,
            "Who is this Polish swine?"
And recall again the reply of Maximilian Kolbe,
            "I am a Catholic priest."

Notice what Father Kolbe did not say. He did not say---
I am Maximilian Kolbe. I am a Pole. I am a human being.
I am a friend of this man.
His response was simply, humble and courageous,

            "I am a Catholic priest."

In the eyes of God; In his own eyes; In the eyes of God's

Church,

Maximilian Kolbe's identity was that of
                                                    a priest.
At the core of his being,
                                    engraved in his heart,
                                    was inscribed a nametag
                                    which marked him forever
                                                    a priest of God.

  In that moment of self-giving,
                                    that moment of trial,
                                    that moment in a hell-hole
which spoke of the total degradation of human life, and
                                    culture and civilization
the priest martyr of 60 years ago identified himself simply:

                        "I am a Catholic priest. "

He had a mind, at that moment, such as Elisha.
In the first reading we see a man of substance called to be a disciple and
assistant by the prophet Elijah.
Now Elisha is well situated!
                                    He has land.
                                    He has 12 pair of oxen.
                                    He has standing in the community.
After the slightest hesitation, Elisha
                                    kills all his oxen
                                    breaks up his plows to build a fire
                                    and prepares a great beef dinner
                                    for his family and friends.

Elisha makes the radical choice to follow the prophet and
                                    he burns all the bridges back to his former life.
Elisha celebrated his radical choice, which cost him everything
                                    but his best self.
Suddenly he was free of all other ties.
His soul and spirit were wafted high on the wind of radical choice.

Father Kolbe and Elisha, in their radical choice, were as Christ in the

gospel we just read:
"When the days for Jesus being taken up were fulfilled,
He resolutely determined to journey to Jerusalem."

Jesus was and is the Eternal Priest...

And He resolutely, with determination and conviction and in total
freedom walked toward the cross.
The moment of total self-giving.
Christ the Eternal Priest identified Himself with the cross of self-giving.

Father Kolbe identified himself with the saving cross.
Father Kolbe, in the moment of radical choice, saw his priestly identity
in the cross of Christ.
He made his own the words of the Responsory of today's Mass,
"You are my inheritance, 0 Lord."
The cross of Christ is the priest's identity and his proper joy.

Father O'Hara, love and cherish the cross of Christ.
The cross is the point of entry into the heart of God.
It will protect you from a loss of
                identity when you
                meet opposition.
It will provide you joy on days when you
                feel saddened by lack of success.
It will give you a profound sense of self-understanding when you
                feel misunderstood.
All human desolation and discouragement has been drawn into the
                Heart of the Trinity.

Father O'Hara, be faithful to the cross on which hung the Salvation
of the World.
Never forget.
        On the cross it was
        Love Itself
                which knew abandonment
                        and desolation.
If you love your life, your God and your people intensely,
Father O'Hara, you must love the cross even more intensely in
order to bear the burden of loving your people
                                and
                                your priesthood.

84

Remember, Jesus never asked that you be successful, as the world
measures success.
Jesus does ask that you be faithful.
Each time you go to the altar
                you hold the broken Body of Christ
                        in your hands
                                and
                        each time you celebrate the sacred event of the
                                Last Supper you say,
                        "This is My body broken for you."
You are acting in the person of Christ at that exalted moment
And it is Christ's Body and His Blood which become present.
But there is another meaning. and another presence as well.
It is your body, your life, your brokenness which you
are offering to God's people.
When you drink of the Precious Blood, you willingly
                put the cup of Christ's suffering to your lips.
This is your identity, Father O'Hara,
and it is in this that you will find your joy
        and your fulfillment as a priest.

"When the days for Jesus being taken up were fulfilled ,
 He resolutely determined to journey to Jerusalem."

Father O'Hara,
In a few days you will be accustomed to being called by the noblest
title a man can have.

You will become accustomed to being called "Father".

Every man wants to see something that he has created.
Most men have that joy when they see their child.
A priest knows that joy when he holds the Eucharistic presence of Christ.
Here is a Life he has pro-created, brought into existence with God's help.

Father O'Hara,
spend time every day in the presence of the life you have co-created.
Spend time before the Lord present in the Eucharist.
Contemplate--- Adore--- Beg--- Rejoice
                        before that Life you have brought into
the world through the power granted to you in the gift of the priesthood.
Father O'Hara,

More will be accomplished there for yourself and for your people
than in many meetings, lectures, sermons, social gatherings,
seminars, study groups.
There too, Father, you will refine and re-fix your identity
                              as a priest -
A man called to give himself to prayer and intercession that God's
mercy be poured out on God's people
                    and your people.
Before the tabernacle, you will learn with total certitude that…
                              the priesthood is---
                              God's greatest gift to man.
Faithfully living the priesthood is---
                              man's greatest gift to God.

Before the tabernacle, you will learn more than from any book
of what is essential.

What is essential and central is that the cross and the crucified Lord
present in the tabernacle remind you to resist the temptation to
compromise with the world.

Our Holy Father has written:
"What people expect of their ordained leaders, is above all a priestly
personality that witnesses to a world beyond this one and to values that
belong to eternity. Priests should not be deceived.
Sometimes the people may want priests to be in every way like them.
At times, it even seems they demand this of us.
A priest must be on his guard.
It is very easy to let oneself be guided by appearances and
fall victim to a fundamental illusion in what is essential.
Those who call for secularization of priest life and applaud its various
manifestations will surely abandon us
if we give in to this temptation.
We shall then cease to be necessary and popular."

The Pope went on to explain how vigilant priests must be to avoid being
manipulated and exploited by a world that wants to shape everyone,
especially the Church's leaders, to its own image and likeness.

Father O'Hara,

Keep your eyes on heroes like Maximilian Kolbe.
Keep your eyes on the cross.
Keep your eyes on the altar
                and the tabernacle
                            and you will never have a problem with
                                    identity or compromise
Today, Father, you have set your face resolutely toward Jerusalem.
If along the way anyone stops you and asks who you are, may you
always have
                the grace
                    the humility
                        the courage to say,

                    "I am a Catholic priest. "

Humility: The Way Of Jesus

No one will dispute with me when I say that one of our greatest presidents was Abraham Lincoln.

This great man had a **disarming ability to laugh at himself** especially his own physical appearance.

When Senator Stephen Douglas once called him a "two faced man" Lincoln responded:

> "I leave it to my audience. If I had
> another face, do you think I would wear
> this one?"

Another time he told of meeting a woman. Lincoln reported:

> "She looked at me and said:
>
> > 'I do believe you are the ugliest man
> > I ever saw.'   Lincoln said:
> >
> > 'Madam, you are probably right but I
> > can't help it.'
>
> 'No,' said the woman, 'You can't help it, but
> you might consider staying at home.' "

Lincoln was humble and hugely effective in his life and death.

The Sacred Scriptures readings today stress **humility.**

> Not a very popular virtue today.

We certainly hear more about self-esteem than we do about humility.

We hear much of self-affirmation and self-fulfillment. How often "**I**", enters into our conversation.

We certainly hear much about individual rights, which amount to a great emphasis on me, the all-important one.

How often do we hear people stressing that they know better than the Pope or Bishop as to how the Church should operate.

What teachings it should change. You have heard it all.
We should have married priests, - they demand.
We should have woman priests, - they demand.
The Church should get into the 21st century
on a whole list of things - they demand.

How much puffing up there is in our
day. How much pride
and arrogance about our own opinions.

The Sacred Scripture says today:

"**My child** conduct your **affairs** with
humility **and you will be loved more
than a giver** of gifts."

"Humble yourselves the more,
the greater you are."

In the Gospel, Jesus tells a parable after He noticed
that people were choosing the places of honor at table.

Jesus says take **the lowest place**. If it's
not the place the host has reserved for you,
you will be called up higher. The humble, will be exalted.

Jesus lived what He preached.

He chose to be born into a carpenter's family.
He chose to be born in a stable.

He chose His friends and disciples from among
unknown fishermen and day laborers.

He chose to **be born** into a **weak, little nation** that
was constantly
on the verge of being wiped out by its big and powerful
neighbors.
When he was born, it was occupied, by the army of Rome.

Such a world shaking and changing mission He had,
yet for 30 of 33 years
He's hidden away,
in a no count town,
working as a village carpenter.
Finally, He chose to be obedient, obedient unto death,
in the most humiliating manner and cruel death,
known to a very cruel world.

If one looks at Christ's life and teaching, we would wonder what was
His favorite virtue?

> Was it **faith** - certainly high up there.
> Was it **hope** - rank it up near the top.
> **Charity** ...think how often the Master spoke of love.

But, all these take second place to **humility.**

HUMILITY is the **pivotal virtue** of the interior life and therefore,
the favorite of Jesus.

It is the virtue, without which, we can
make no progress in the interior life.

St. Therese of Lisieux said:

> "The beginning of all holiness is humbly
> admitting that without God we can do nothing
> but that, with, in and through Him
> all things are possible."

The Gospels are odes to humility.

On every page we see the divine preferences for

The humble,
The sick over the healthy.
The poor over the rich.
The lowly virgin over the high visibly socialite.
The oafish fisherman over the educated
    scribes and Pharisees.
The nerds over the in-crowd.
The sinners over the smug and self-satisfied.
Children over adults.

"Lord, I am not worthy" admits the centurion.

"Just the scraps from the table" begs the
Canaanite woman.

"Lord remember me when you come into your kingdom," pleads the
thief on the cross.

All these humble prayers and petitions
touched and moved the Sacred Heart of the One
who said of Himself
    "I am gentle and lowly
    of heart."

Why was humility so prized by Christ? Maybe because
His whole mission was to save us from the
opposite vice--- pride.
    the original sin by which
    our first parents thought they
    could get along just fine
    without God.

We know what a mess that pride brought
into the world - all the wars,
    murders,
    crimes of every sort of every age up to
    September 11, 2001.

Sadness, unending, flows from that original pride.
Humility helps us to recognize that every thing we have is gift.

This Labor day weekend speeches long and short
will be made about the huge productivity of
our work force and our nation.

Let us hope there
is room for some humility in those speeches.

May the speakers not forget that we were gifted with a nation
mostly in the temperate zone and so
agriculture is hugely productive.
Good growing weather,
                    rain,
                    sunshine,
                    fertile soil.
                    All are gifts.

            Our land was filled with enormous natural
                    resources
            and the greatest of all - an
                    industrious,
                    enterprising,
                    risk-taking people---
                    human capital, that knew what
                    to do with a naturally rich
                    huge expanse of rich land and great rivers and fresh
water lakes.

                    Each human life - a gift.

Let us be humble people, gentle, caring,
prepared to give deference to others
            and all credit to God.

When all is said and done, the project of life is to become
a saint. - A saint finds God in this life and the next.

The road to holiness is marked out clearly.

            St Augustine said: "If you ask me the
                    three ways to God I would tell you the
                    first is humility, the second is humility,
                    the third
                    is humility."

The way of humility and the
way of God are illustrated at every Mass.
We begin by humbly admitting
our sin.

"Lord have mercy, Christ have mercy, Lord have mercy".

Then
        a tiny bit of bread
        a few ounces of wine

                are God's chosen little,
                humble ways to come to
                us in the fullness of His
                life and power, salvation and the

                promise of heaven.

That is the humility of God.
It must be met by our own
humility when with faith we say

                      "My Lord and my God,

                      have mercy on me..."

My Mother's Funeral

To our aunts and uncles,
          cousins, nephews, nieces,
          relatives and friends,
my brothers and sisters and I wish
to thank you for your presence
in sharing our grief as we share yours.

Bernie could never go anywhere without
his beloved and jealously guarded Kate but, this is a bit much.
He did not need to demand
his beautiful Valentine, our mother,
                    sister,
                          grandmother
                          great-grandmother,
                    join him on the first Valentine's
                    day after his death only 4 weeks ago.

I wonder, do we believe in signs,
                    in strange coincidences,
                    in subtle hints.

Let me share some signs, subtle hints, some mysteries of life
                                        with Mother
                                        and Dad.

In the late 1940's Mother and Dad
built a beautiful home for their growing family.

Mother was a lover of trees, royal red maples, ginkgos,
                          lindens,
                          birch.

Several royal red maples were planted around the
new home. They prospered, slowly,
                                    beautifully in the way
                                    of royal red maples.
In 1972 Mother and Dad moved to the
farm where they lived the last
30 years of their lives.

Mother insisted that one of the royal reds go
to the new home.

It was arranged – the big tree spade came
by and one of Mother's beloved maple got
a place of honor at the new home.

How many times I came by on a July or August
afternoon and Mother or Dad, one or both
would be sitting in the deep shade of their friendly maple---
usually the family dog would be there as well – domestic peace and
tranquility.

   About 2 years ago Dad began experiencing his first health problems.
   About 2 years ago the royal red maple began to show signs of
                                                      weakness.

      This past summer the maple tree was a
      sickly thing – so few leaves
                     its shade offered almost
                     no relief from the hot sun
                     the lawn chairs were not even put beneath the
              tree this past summer.

                     It was the summer Dad was not well at all.
      It was the summer Mother was wearing herself out
                     in one final, sensitive gesture of sacrificial love
                                                      and caring
                                                      for her
                                                      husband of 68
                                                      years.

              The maple tree lost all its leaves before the
              first frost – it was a very sick tree and old.

95

One day when Mother had taken Dad
to see a doctor, again, I cut that tree down.

I worked on the large stump until nothing remained
above ground level.
Now winter's snow hides that scar on the earth.

 This spring a few shovels of dirt, a handful of seed and
only memory will remain of the
beautiful maple.

And like wise, only memory will remain of those
beautiful ones who sat, often holding
hands, under the royal red maple.

Strange and beautiful coincidence
that the royal red sickened and died at the same time
those who
loved it and rested
in its shade sickened and died.

When I saw Mother and Dad
under that tree, I occasionally recalled the
times we would be driving
Hwy 33 going to or coming from
grandma's house in La Crosse
in an old Plymouth.
Two handsome people in the front
seat would be singing – both loved
to sing and did it well.
It was WWII time and
one song they sang went:
"Don't sit under the apple tree
with anyone else but me
anyone else but me
anyone else but me.
Don't sit under the apple tree
With anyone else but me
Till I
come
marching home." - They accepted the request
and now both

have marched home almost in lock step
and we pray they sit together
under heaven's equivalent of an apple
                                    tree.

Do you believe in signs?
          In portents?
          In hints of hidden
          meanings
          beyond the ordinary.
          There are those among us who saw what
          others did not see.

Some of her daughters reported that Friday morning
          while the first of many rosaries of the day
          was in progress

               Mother straightened up
                    her eyes opened wide and
               she said
                    " I see her."
          "Who mother? Who do you see?"

               "I see the Blessed Mother."

Do you believe in signs?

I will make no point of that moment except
 to report what has been told me. Maybe that is too much.

But it is significant that in her final hours
          Mother would report a vision, a sign,
                    of life not death;
                    of beauty not ugliness;
                    of joy not sadness;
                    of hope not despair;
                    of faith not unbelief.

That manner of vision was Mother's vision of
 living
               and for that reason she set a high
               bar for herself and she set a high
               bar for her children.

And in her living, Mother cleared the high bar in so many ways.

First and with every fiber Catherine Hundt was a Christian
Catholic mother.
Mother worried about her impact in life.

She worried out loud to a grandson with whom she
especially loved to talk.

One day she said – "I want to give my kids a
special gift but I don't know what it could be.

> They have educations,
> nice homes,
> good partners,
> they are successful.

What do I give them?

One day while praying the rosary, my mind
was suddenly at peace over that question.

It came to me, I have given them a
love for the Catholic faith – all eleven –
what greater gift could I possibly give –
every other gift would only be for a time –
> this love for their faith is
> a gift that keeps on giving –
> forever."

Like the words of the Old Testament figure,

Mother was the one who said with her life
"Here I am Lord
> I have heard You
> calling in the night.
> > I will go Lord
> if You lead me.
> > I will hold Your
> people in my heart."

"Finest bread I will provide till their hearts be satisfied."

"I will give my life to them"

How many times this good mother heard the
voice of the Lord in one of the children calling to
her in the night.
> Without reservation her response was
> > "I will hold Your people in
> > my heart." And she held her kids
> > in her heart and in her arms
> > as the little ones and not so little ones
> > experienced the illnesses and fears of
> > childhood and beyond.

Do we believe in signs?

This good and precious woman believed with all
her heart the signs which spoke to her of
a new and greater life, signs with inner power and mysterious meaning.

She believed in the sign of water by which
she and her children received the
promise of eternal life.
> She, with Dad, presented 13 children in this temple
> on the hill to receive the gift of New Life
> > the eternal, invisible watermark
> designating Mother and Mother's children
> > as God's children forever.

This good woman believed in signs – the sign of freshly baked bread
spoke to her of love,
> dedication,
> caring,
> and yes, good eating.

The splendid, intoxicating odor of Mother's baking was almost a
perpetual presence in her home.
Her bread was
essential and central
to every meal.

Mother believed in signs. The sign of bread which Christ left us
was most dear to her.
> She accepted without reservation

that the bread of the Eucharist was not
bread but was truly and really the
Body of Christ.

She accepted without reservation
that to eat the bread Christ provided
was to have Eternal Life in her.

So many thousands of times she came
to the table of the Lord to receive the bread
of Eternal Life.

Mother believed in signs. She believed in the sign of the
imposition of hands on her eldest son's head.

By that he was priest – she was mother of a
priest – there by entering a very special rank of woman.
Now she was instrumental every
day in preparing the bread for the
special family of God.
Through her priest son
she was baker for a much wider
family and an even more precious bread.
Bread, truly
"out of this
world" good.
Dear Mother lived the words she
knew so well.

This is My Body,
My love,
My energy,
My heart,
My everything given for

you.

These words spoke the motto of her life – she lived the
mystery she believed and received.

Hundreds of times I gave
Holy Communion to Mother.

100

Because of her gift of temporal life to me
I could give the gift of Eternal Life to her,

a wondrous joy every day,
a wondrous consolation today,
a wondrous mystery
of God's love and mother's love
intertwined
and focused
in one humble
and blinding moment
of temporal and
eternal truth.

Yes, truly on this mountain, the Lord destroys
the web that is woven over all
nations.

In her early years and her later
she was a woman of much prayer –
a woman devoted
to the Blessed Mother.

Around her bed we sang many times a
beautiful hymn to Mary.
"Gentle woman, quiet light
so strong and bright
gentle mother
peaceful dove,
teach us wisdom
teach us love."

I confess and I will not deny…
I cried every time we sang those words
because they seemed so befitting the
woman who
lay stricken before us

A strong,
bright,
peaceful

dove
who had
taught us
wisdom
had taught us
love.

Her artistry was not only in paint and oil,
in shadows and proper composition,
in world class bread ,
in Sunday chicken dinners beyond
compare,
in beautiful flower gardens,
or
nicely arranged rooms.

She did those all well

but best she was an artist in
shaping the lives of her children and she did it so well
because she prayed so much and loved so deeply.

She was the strong and valiant woman of whom
the Sacred Scripture says

"Happy the husband of a good wife.

happy the children of a good mother."

She was the quiet light so strong and bright.

But the light we loved,
in whose presence we flourished
has now returned
to the source of all Light,
from whence 85 years ago she came.

Like a good candle in a dark place
Mother, Kate has burned bright and true.
But the wax is spent,
the day is done.

About two weeks ago Mother was being driven
home from yet another trip to the doctor.

As they came down the driveway the family
home was just a darker shadow in the gathering
gloom of night.

Mother said – "I want some of those things that
turn lights on automatically, I
want light in my house when I
come home at night."

Well, Mother, your truly wonderful
journey is finished, it was a grand tour,
you finished at night's
darkest hour
and

our prayer is that when you approached the
home of your spiritual friends
Padre Pio

Sister Faustina

the Blessed Mother

Our dear Lord…

our prayer is that the lights were all on and

Dad gave you a Valentines Day

embrace.

Deliver Us From Evil

After the turmoil,
    the confusion,
    the sadness and shock of this week,
    it is comforting to be here.

    Here, where predictable words are spoken,
        predictable actions done,
        well known songs sung,
    where there is a predictable beginning, middle and end of
    what we do,
        and where the homily is predictably long.

We heard of people making calls to mothers
        husbands
        wives for comfort
        and love in the face
        of certain death this past week.

Mother Church in her ancient yet always new presence gathers us to herself this morning in this building where we hear again the words of comfort that have pierced through every crisis moment great and small for 2000 years.

The **Lord of history** and **Lord** of **life** and **death** saying to us again this morning: "This is My body, My life given for you. Remember – I am with you all days until the end of the world."

On **Thursday** morning, very early, I picked up my breviary.

It was eerie what priests around the country and the world were reading that morning, Thursday morning, 48 hours
        after Tuesday's attack.

Listen, this is some of what they and others read from
the Old Testament.

> "How lonely she is now,
> the once crowded city,
> widowed is she
> who was mistress over nations.

> Bitterly she weeps at night.
> Tears upon her cheeks.
> Her persecutors come upon her
> Where she is narrowly confined.

> Gone is her glory.

> Her people fell into **enemy** hands.

> Her foes **gloated** over her and
> **laughed** at her ruins.

Come, all you who pass by the way,
> look and see,
> Whether there is any suffering like my suffering
Which has been dealt to me."

All of this was written, firstly about Jerusalem in a period if its history
(about 600 years before Christ) when it was devastated – its people and
the whole nation humiliated,

forced into exile into the region of present day Iraq,
but God's Word is for all ages and all cities and so they speak
to us this morning as they will through the next weeks and months.

One morning, I believe Friday, a woman of the parish
came to me after Mass and said:
> "Father, I have been saying the Lord's
> prayer for 70 years
> > but
> this morning, for the first time, it exploded
> in me that there is one petition which I have
> never taken seriously enough."

> "Oh yes? And which one is it?" , I asked.
> "Deliver us from evil" she said.

"Deliver us from evil" indeed!

This Tuesday past evil was delivered to us.
        Evil exploded in our cities and our countryside.
        Evil had its day and its way.
        Evil changed our lives and our nation.
        Evil has cursed us with the reality of war.

For any who wonder if evil exists, this particular Tuesday
should have dispelled all doubt.

For those who argue that evil is only such, "if I think it is" -
well, we have crumbled
towers and thousands of deaths
proving evil is an objective reality.
        Yet those who did those things
        did so in the name of their god -
in their twisted minds they are heroic martyrs.
        Moral relativism is the first and most deadly terrorism.

President Bush has said in these last days:

        "We must rid the world of evil."

No one, I hope will argue with the President's
rhetorical flourish. **In the crisis** of the **moment** he has
        a **speaker's license**
        to say that.

But, the simple and distressing truth is

        we humans will never rid the world
        of evil.

Brave decision makers of our government,
Brave men and women of our military,
Great sums of our treasury and industry
        will stamp out in due time one
        particularly ugly brand of evil.

But we will not rid the world of evil.

We are dealing with
sin in its grossest form.
The second reading says
"Jesus Christ came into the world to save sinners."
Only Christ can rid the world of evil.

Dear friends, on this somber Sunday

we must look to that central moment
of all human history. The truly history changing moment
when it seemed as though hatred,
 death,
 insanity had won the day
over
life,
love,
reason.

On a Friday long ago,
Our Savior and Lord died on the cross because
of hatred and a kind of insanity.

That crucifixion moment has come to
our land, to cities and countryside.

Hatred,
Death,
Insanity had their obscene, victorious moments.

But life,
love
and human dignity are stronger and will
prevail. God Himself decreed such.
God Himself, in Jesus, lived that death and resurrection cycle and from
that we take our hope and comfort.

As for ridding the world of evil –
let us look into ourselves
and re-commit our lives to Christ,
mold our hearts to the Sacred heart,
put on the mind of Christ which was,

first of all, a mind and will given to
total obedience to the will of the Father.
Then at least our personal world may be rid of evil.

Let us pray fervently for our nation,
our president and his team,
our military leadership and all
military personnel present and future,
our people in homes,
offices,
factories
and farms across the nation.

Let us not be afraid!

Let us be kind
comforting
encouraging
generous
peaceful with those closest to us
and those who are strangers.

Let us turn most especially to God during this
time of trial which is with us and lies before us.

Let us pray for the overwhelming conviction that God's
peace plan for the world is a person - Jesus

The Lord of History
The Savior
The One in Whom all things
hold together.

And let us pray that the words
spoken firstly of ancient Jerusalem never be applicable to a
city of our land.

The words which say:

"Bitterly she weeps at night.
Tears upon her cheeks.

Come, all you who pass by the way
look and see
whether there is any suffering like my suffering
which has been dealt to me."

"Almighty and merciful God, you cannot be understood by
the one who sows hatred,
you cannot be accepted by the one who loves violence;
look upon
our painful human condition,
tried by cruel acts of terror and death;
comfort your children and open our hearts to hope,
so that our time can
know days of serenity and peace." (Pope John Paul II)

Patriotism:
The Christian Value

This past week has been a celebration of America over-riding
                                  the tears and fears.
We realize, even in the midst of terrorist tragedy
we have so much to celebrate.

We **celebrate the steel strong bravery** evidenced by so many
coming from a society which has been criticized as being
soft and squishy.

We **celebrate** the outpouring of **generosity** of people, with
          their money
          their time
          their blood.
                    And all this from a society which
                    has often been called **selfish.**

We **celebrate** the society, which has seen millions, upon
millions in churches
          mosques
          synagogues
                    in a society which has often
                    been called **Godless**.

We **celebrate** the **goodness** gushing
from Americans in the face of unspeakable evil
poured out on our homeland.

We **celebrate** the **great unity** among us in
a land which also prizes **diversity.**

From the halls of congress
        to beer halls
        to Cathedrals and ball parks
                praise of American ideals,
                thankfulness for the wonder of the
                        American experiment in government
instituted to protect the freedom and dignity of all

                has filled the airways,
                the shopping malls,
                the barber shops and golf courses of our land.

You may think this is an unworthy or out of place
speech for the Church.

Notice the first words of the great St. Paul.

Maybe its important to remember he wrote the
words we read to a bishop, not a church.

Paul says: "Bishop Timothy,

                I ask that prayers
                        petitions
                        thanksgiving

                be offered for kings and all in authority
                that we may lead a quiet and tranquil
                life of dignity and devotion.
                This is pleasing to God our Savior."

Pray, Paul says to us, pray for your president
                your legislators
                your military
                your decision makers
Pray for those who carry for a time the heavy
                        heavy
                burden of serving the people's needs
                to live in a country that is safe from
                its external enemies and peaceful in its own
                        borders.

This week we celebrated the **virtue** of **patriotism.**

Patriotism is a virtue that comes under the
4th Commandment.

    We generally hear that Commandment

        "Honor your father and mother."

But we also hear of **Mother**land
           Fatherland
   homeland.

As we honor those who gave us physical
life so we honor our country

    who like a father or mother or home

        has given us a way of life
        a national identity
        a place in the world.

Our country is not perfect - none are.

Each of **us** is guilty of sin, small or great,
in our own way.
    But the imperfections of our country

        or

        of ourselves and others
        can wait for another day
        for the attention they might deserve.

In the mean time we will display our flag in Church
        and on the front door of the
        parish house.

In this time of continuing crisis we will speak of
courage
hope
self-sacrifice
faith and trust in God
freedom
    lived, loved, preserved.

We have heard many words on how we should respond
to the changed situation in which we find ourselves.

Some of the advice we hear doesn't go far enough.

> Without faith in God Who **is very good**
> there is no way to face a world which can be **very evil**.

I suggest that Our Holy Father Pope John Paul II
offers us an example to follow.

Today that old and weakened man is in Kazakhstan and Armenia.

A world in crisis has not stopped him from making
yet another mission to a land where only
1.2% of the people are Catholic.

He goes to present to all who will listen the
ancient but ever new message that God's
peace plan for the world is a person,

> Jesus, Son of God and Son of Mary.

Jesus passed through the valley of death to new life.

If now we find ourselves in the valley of death let
us live the God-given hope and trust that
Christ the Good Shepherd with all the love in
His divine Heart will
lead us through the valley of death to new life.

> It is not, cannot be, His will that we find **a permanent**
> residence in the valley of death anymore than He did.

This, dear friends, is a time to trust the leadership of
our nation and love its people and cities
> its mountains and rivers
> its fertile planes and valleys
> its vast expanses from sea to shining sea.

But, **more importantly still** we must turn to that One
Who did what no mere man
                        no great army
                        no homeland security force can do.

Jesus fought against the forces of death and won.

DRAW near to Him - Sunday mass each week with the
                        family and more often if possible.

                -    confession
                -    prayer at home
                -    the rosary of Our Lady.

We are in a battle, which, will be decided on the front
of the spiritual
                        what armies
                                special forces
                                air marshals
                                security checks
                and armadas of ships and planes accomplish

                        are efforts only of mopping up
                        after the spiritual battle is won.

When all turn to serve Christ with all their heart and
                                                soul
                                life and energy

                Then the battle will be over.

Let us imagine the flashes of light high in the Twin Towers
                as wake up calls.

                A call to turn fully to Christ the light of the
                world.
                And some day we might see that
                                great and **lasting** good

                        that came from horrendous and
                        passing evil.

The light in the towers produced unfathomable death and misery,
darkness and sadness.

The light, which is Christ, produces only
life and joy
peace and security.

In these troubles of ours
be patriotic - love your country
In these troubles of ours
be fully and totally a Catholic, Christian.

LOVE CHRIST ABOVE ALL.

Mary's YES
Set The World Upside Down

Our Christian faith is a mystery and a challenge.

We always seem to be faced with things turned
upside down.

Consider today's feast.

> An unknown girl in an unknown town is born
> to unknown parents.

They call her Mary.

She grows up and one day a heavenly messenger
comes to her and says:

"Hail, full of grace, the Lord is with you."

From that phrase, we get the teaching
> the doctrine of the
> > Immaculate Conception.

She is **full of grace,** there is no trace
of sin in her.

She is **full of grace** she can not carry any of the
effects of original sin.

She is **perfect** with the perfection only an infinite God
could give her.

She is the perfect mother prepared for a
perfect Son - Jesus.

And her perfection is **unknown** to all but God and His **messenger.**

That already turns all the wisdom and ways of the
world on its head.

The wisdom of the world would say such a
person should be known to all.
He should be living in one of the power centers of the
world - not scroungy little Palestine in unknown
Nazareth.

Then the angel says, **"Blessed are you"**

Mary was blessed - specially sanctified and chosen by God.

What did her blessing get her?

She was blessed with an unexpected teenage
pregnancy.
She was blessed to give birth in an animal shelter
without a midwife.
She was blessed to live in **poverty.**
She was blessed to see her Son become a homeless
preacher and beggar.
She was blessed to see her only Son abandon the
family business.
She was blessed to see her Son preach some strange
things which changed drastically her beloved and
ancient religion.

She was blessed to see her Son ridiculed,
falsely accused, tortured
and
killed as a criminal.
She was blessed to hold her lifeless Son in her arms.

She who was blessed,
> specially chosen, specially
> prepared.

Everything is **set on its head**
> upside down
> inside out according to the wisdom of
> the world.

But, all this is the wisdom and the plan of God.

We ought think on these things in regard to more common things
in Catholic Life.

When confession to a priest doesn't make human sense…
Remember it makes **God sense** and that's what matters.

When a bit of bread and wine changed into the
Body and Blood of Christ doesn't make human sense…
Remember it makes **God sense** and that's what matters.

When your life seems turned on its head by discouragement,
> suffering,
> abandonment,
> loneliness,
> confusion…

Remember the blessed one of today's feast and you may
discover the wisdom of God
> and
> pray for the grace to say "yes" as she did.

For in all her trials God did not abandon Mary and
> He will not abandon you.

Aunt Evelyn ~ Humble, Simple

I begin this morning with words of sympathy
and consolation to
               sister Caroline,
               brother Dave,
                             to nieces and nephews
                                        other relatives and friends.

When Aunt Evelyn's death became known to various
members of the family, a refrain became common.

I heard from 3 different sources who spoke
independently.

"Poor Evelyn, she sort of fell through the cracks of life"

               She sort of fell through the cracks.

I wonder, family, friends…

I wonder if that is not precisely, right-on-the-
money wrong.

I saw Evelyn quite frequently these past
15-18 years.

               Not infrequently dear Mother would
               journey to West Salem to bring Ev
               to the Farm for a few hours.

                    Brother Mark was generous in doing that
                    as well.

Now what did I observe when I saw Ev…

I saw one who was meek and humble.

I saw one who was detached from the things of this world.
$$-money,$$
$$car,$$
$$possessions\ meant\ almost$$
$$nothing\ to\ her.$$

I saw one who was almost always cheerful.

I saw one mostly peaceful with the world around her.

I saw one who made no harsh judgments
about others.
One who had no enemies.

I saw one who could sit and watch the leaves
blow in the wind and be mostly
content.

I saw one who knew no envy,
no greed,
no lust,
no prejudice,
no arrogance of mind
or
spirit.

I saw one who was the little child of the Sacred Scriptures, simple
trusting, good.

The one who was a believer.
one who lived with hope in Eternal Life
one who loved God and neighbor.

I saw one who had the watermark of
Baptism upon her... "We who were baptized
into Christ Jesus
were baptized into His death so that
just as Christ was raised from the dead
by the glory of the Father
we too might live in newness of life."

Now I wonder – is this one who could

possibly fall through the cracks?
Our vision is too short if we see in Ev an
inhabitor of the cracks of life.
What is the purpose of life?

What really and truly is the purpose of life – a
purpose which if you attain it you not only
 don't fall into the cracks but you rise to
the pinnacle of perfection and fulfillment.

The purpose of life according to God's own
Word
                              To know and love God in this life
                                              and
                      to be happy with Him in heaven.

Now it seems to me that if we have one
whose life
looked like an illustration of the
Sermon on the Mount we should not worry
about one whose life has fallen into the cracks.

Was not Ev one of those child-like to whom
the Father revealed the mysteries of His love –
things hidden from the wise or the learned.

          Ev had no problem believing the
          words of John's Gospel where Jesus says

              "My flesh is real food, My blood is
              real drink. Whosoever eats My flesh and drinks
              My blood remains in Me and I in him. Whosoever
              eats this bread will live forever."

Whosoever eats **this** bread will live forever.

          With such a promise from the Lord can it ever
          be said
                    such a one falls through the cracks
                    of life.

Is it
not entirely
more likely that
in the **eternal scheme**
of things each of us here
is more likely than Ev to fall into
the cracks of life.

It is God's eternal plan to use the meek and humble for
great purposes.

> The humble maid of Nazareth became
> God's mother.
> The humble cave in Bethlehem became
> God's birthplace on earth.
> The humble carpenter's home became
> the dwelling place of God on earth for
> 30 years or more.
> The humble bit of bread
> would be turned into Christ's body.
> The humble bit of wine would be turned into Christ's
> blood.

The humble fishermen of Palestine would become missionaries
to the world.

The One neglected by the builders became
the cornerstone of the building.

The humble never fall through the cracks of life when
God takes hold of them.

> They accomplish the purpose God
> has in mind for them and are by
> that raised up,
> > exalted,
> > eternally crowned with glory in
> > the Church of heaven.

Ev was one of the meek and humble
of the earth.

> She did not fall through the cracks in God's
> plan and when all is said and done that's the

only plan that counts because it's the
only plan with eternal depth and meaning.

We want to thank those of Lakeview Health Care Center
who cared for Ev so long and so well
                and
Kate, the mother of so many of us here
was a devoted,
        concerned,
        caring
                guardian to Ev.

I'm certain when Mother appeared before Our Lord
He said "When I was sick you visited me."
It is only our ancient Christian faith that can shed
a consoling,
        comforting light on a life such as Ev's
                on a day such as today,

                but our faith is real and alive
                        and
                therefore our comfort
                        and
                consolation is real
                on a day such as today.

Confessions...Come

Yesterday we celebrated the Solemnity of the Immaculate
Conception of Mary.
That means that Mary was conceived without sin.

There was a time when Catholics were ridiculed for believing that Mary,
one person,
the Mother of God, was totally free from sin.

Now the Church is ridiculed for believing that only one and not everyone
is free from sin.
One hears so much today about people
searching for a spiritual life, for exclusive holiness.

People look all over the place for a new spiritual guru, a new system,
> new ideas,
> new religion,
> new parish.

One of the **glories** of our Church is that it has produced
an army of **saintly people, spiritual masters and teachers and guides.**

> One characteristic, common to all the saints
> was their humble recognition and
> acknowledgement that before the majesty and
> holiness of God they were miserable sinners.

> > This humility prompted them to take John's
> > words, which we read today seriously, very
> > seriously.

"Repent, do penance, the Kingdom of God is at hand."

The humble recognition of their sinfulness
made the saints
great lovers of the sacrament of penance.

The Little Flower, the beloved St. Therese of Lisieux, wrote that the humble recognition of our sinfulness and an acceptance of God's infinite mercy in the sacrament of penance is the beginning of all holiness, all true spiritual life.

A very saintly man died just a year ago. His name,
Fr. John Hardon. One evening, after a dinner at which
about 400 people were present, I met Fr. Hardon.

He came up to me - He asked that I hear
his confession.
I said "Fine," "Where?" He said

"Right here."

So with the crowd moving by
we had this intimate moment
while a humble sinner, far into
his 80's bared his soul.
When we finished a person
helping the feeble old man
came up to me and said,

"Fr. Hardon has gone to confession **every day** for
53 years."

When is the last time we went to confession?
Do you know of Fr. Damien Veuster?

He was a man from Belgium who left his comfortable home
and country
for the life of a missionary.
He ended in Molokai, the leper colony in the Hawaiian Islands.

After 25 years someone asked him what was the most difficult thing
about his missionary life?
Was it 25 years away from home?
Was it 16 of those 25 years spent
with the lepers?
Was it contracting leprosy himself?
Was it the pain of being unjustly

accused of moral wrongdoing?

According to his own testimony the heaviest cross
to carry was the impossibility of frequent
confession since no other priest could come
to the island of Molokai.

> Imagine--- with all the other
> suffering or pain he had to
> bear... the greatest was being
> deprived   of   frequent
> confession.

This man is officially designated as a

saint of the Church.

When was the last time we went to

confession?

The warning to "Repent" was God's
word burning into Damien's sensitive
soul.

> He needed,
> > wanted
> > > to hear the words of
> > > absolution
> > > from a priest.

> Those words would assure him his sins
> were forgiven.

Would we say the greatest pain in life is
lacking
a chance for frequent confession?
The saints, our models, felt this way.
We search for God because we
search to find meaning and
purpose in our lives---
Especially we want to live
forever!
So, we search for that font of
youth which will satisfy our
desire to live forever.

God is the source of all life. God is the source
of the font of eternal youth.

Where do we find Him?

We find Him in the Child of Bethlehem,
          the Wonder Worker of Nazareth,
          the Crucified and Risen One.
So we are like the woman who was sick for 38 years. A
lifetime in her day.

 She sees Jesus and she says to herself - if only I could
touch Him or at least **touch the hem of His** cloak - I'd be healed.

Notice - she had to **touch something -** come into
physical contact with Jesus.

Salvation comes through the body, senses - that
has been true since the day God took on a
physical body. God-in-the-flesh explains so much about the
practices of our beautiful faith.

A spiritual life that doesn't include material, physical, bodily
contact with Christ is dangerous day dreaming and is really
denial that God lived a human life in Jesus.

The question is…

How do we do that? How can we reach out and touch Jesus?

"Don't you know," St. Paul says, **"that the Church is the Body of Christ."**

We touch the healing, infinitely merciful Lord in the sacrament of confession.

> This is where we reach out to touch the
> Lord, to heal us of
> the life long sickness of soul,
> that can and will rob us of eternal
> life and our desire to live forever may be
> eternally frustrated.

"Repent !", John the Baptist urges us today.

> The single **greatest sadness** in the Church life over the past 30-40 years is the near **disappearance of the sacrament of penance -** it's a spiritual catastrophe for individuals and for the Church.

> **With that** comes the disappearance of sin.

> **With that** has come the appearance of so many
> unworthy and sacrilegious Communions.
> **With that** has come the sentiment of
> "I'm OK-You're OK"
> and it's only a sentiment, not a reality.

> > **With that** thinking we destroy a need
> > for a Savior and we tell God that those who said
> > a God-in-the-flesh and a
> > Crucified Savior was a foolish
> > absurdity were, **after all,**
> > correct.

> > **When did we go to confession last?**

I remember telling a little boy after his first
Confession...

"You did very well, next time it will be much
easier."

and the little boy asked

"You mean I have to do this again?"

I smiled and sent him on his way...

Yes, my son, again and again and again until that day
you will not need God's mercy but will have passed
beyond the possibility of sin
you will have died and hopefully achieved
eternal life.

But---until that time - Yes! Again, and Again and Again. Until death.

When did you last go to confession?

Snapshots of a Family Christmas

I hope your Christmas celebration was rich in family activity.

I can tell you mine was.
How is it possible to be otherwise
when ten brothers and sisters gather in the big farm house of a brother ?
> Ten blessed…
> > to have a still active set of parents to anchor
> > the holiday celebration.

As usual the sisters and sisters-in-law took care of the
meal preparation which this year featured a home
grown turkey which weighed in at 37 lbs.

The male contingent could look forward to the
clean-up duties.

A brother-in-law who has a ten-year tradition of carving the turkey
remarked that a project that size allowed room for two to carve.
He did it alone.

Many Christmas carols were sung as the final preparations
were made.
> A nephew home from school in Bulgaria got
> the group to harmonizing.
> An assortment of good pre-dinner wines helped the singing along.

> Toddlers and small children
> held stuffed animals by an ear or a new toy
> and actually quieted down <u>watching and listening</u> as
> their parents, uncles, aunts and cousins sang.

After the slow, long dinner a football game

in the snow for those young and brave enough - I wasn't one of those.
Then about 7:00 in the evening we all gathered at my parents home
for another tradition,
the lighting of the big bon fire in the hollow down the hill from the
family home.
At the center of this fire was last year's
Christmas trees. of the family and many neighbors.

There were some carols of Christmas again and finally
as the fire burned down
to a mound of coals the group started up
the hill to the home.

Now it was time for wonderful venison
sausage, another round of wine and finding
a chair in the over-full home.

Gradually the final Merry Christmas greetings of
the departing were heard. Christmas day had
been fully celebrated.

But, this year Christmas day did not
end the celebration.
On the day after Christmas we gathered at
St. Peter's, in Middle Ridge.

A sister had suggested a Mass.
It was a time to reflect on the centrality of marriage and family.
There was a blessing for all married couples.

That was followed by yet **another** big dinner
at the same brother's home where we had the Christmas feast.
I think of my Christmas experience today
on the feast of the Holy Family.
I hope yours was as rich.

Recently, **I read something** about the giant sequoia trees
in California.
One would think those huge trees had an
enormously deep root system.
The truth is their roots are shallow.

What keeps them standing is that the sequoia trees grow in **groves,** in families of trees.

Their shallow roots intertwine.

When the powerful California winds blow the **trees hold each other up.**

Is not that which makes a family strong? Intertwined lives

intertwined

roots.

When a tragedy or difficulty comes to one,
the family is there to hold up the one affected
by serious problem or sadness.

The feast of the Holy Family reminds us powerfully
of several things.

First, the family is a school of **holiness.**
What else could it mean that God chose to live in
a human family.
Every family in which Christ is the true center
is a holy family.
Second, the family is **primary.**

Jesus came to do some very important things.
Yet He spent 30 years hidden away in family life in Nazareth.

He spent 3 years doing the things we
read about in the Gospel most
Sundays and weekdays of the year.

Do the math 30 years at home.
Three years in
public.
Ten times as many years with
family as with the public.

Third, remember, **family** is
God's design.

It's   not   the   result   of
patriarchal   or   cultural
imposition, as some people
stridently insist in our day.
Family is part of the natural law
engraved in our spirits by the
                              Author of nature,
     by God, Himself.

The feast of the Holy Family is rather new.
About 125 years ago people became concerned
about the break down of family life.

In 1921 this feast of the Holy Family was
extended to the whole Church.

If the family was in trouble in 1875 or 1921, what do
we call its condition now?

Divorce and out of wed-lock births are an epidemic.

The institution of the modern family
has fallen back
to its sorry state before Christianity.

An explosion of individual rights
tears away at the marriage bond and family unity.

          The intertwined roots which make families
                         strong
          are being cut apart so that each individual can
          and must
          stand alone against the winds and trials of life.
                              And how many are
          blown down ?! !

The readings of today speak of honor and respect
children owe parents.

          Of the diligent, self-sacrificing love
          parents owe children.

And St. Paul says to all:

"Dear and beloved friends put on

kindness,

humility, gentleness, patience;

Forgive one another
And over all these
put on love, which
bind
the rest together."

Put on love, which intertwines the roots of
family members so that all might stand against
the roaring winds which blow against the
family
and individual members of the family.

Joined together in love, joined together in faith,
prayer
and the Holy Sacrament of the Eucharist
the family can
endure all.

Earl Gees ~
One Of The Great Generation

First of all this morning a word of sympathy and
consolation to Tom and Ann,
        to Lucille,
            granddaughters,
              nieces,
              nephews
              other relatives
                    and
              many friends.

Tom, it is a hard moment when one
comes to this day of dad's funeral.

           "O, my papa~
           to me you were
           so wonderful."

It is totally fitting to **weep** over
Dad's death,
        to **cherish** his memory,
        treasure his ring, or watch,
        or favorite putter;
        remember his stories, mannerisms, likes
                          and dislikes.

But, thankfully, we can
come to this day with an insight which is
so wonderfully comforting.

        In the Christian context, what we
        see before us is almost illusion.

The body lies in death.
>   Dad **lives** with the gift of the
>   new life Christ won for us who
>   face the certitude of death.

Lucille, it is the most bitter of moments to bury a
>   husband,
>   friend,
>   lover,
>   confidant,
>   soul-mate,
>   life partner.

This is the one who thrilled your young spirit
when he asked you to marry him.

Your Earl gave you the beautiful title – Mother.

Earl loved you well
>   and you loved him well
>   >   and
>   >   so you knew 57 years of marriage.

Remember, Lucille, a day like today,
sad as it is,
has this great positive note.

>   Your life pact with Earl,
>   your life commitment to your husband
>   is forever sealed

>   >   forever Earl will be
>   >   yours and
>   >   you, his.

Let the warm light of a love you knew,
>   a love you lived,
>   a love you treasured,
>   a love you can never lose
remove some of the bitterness of this day.

Earl had three other precious ladies in his life.

His three princesses,
Jennifer,
Katie,
Christie.

Cherish the memory of your Grandfather, girls.

Cherish the fact that you had a grandfather who
was one of that special group of Americans
who have come to be called …
the Great Generation.

The Great Generation faced a great crisis
from **inside**
the country called the
"Great Depression" and won.

The Great Generation faced a great crisis
from enemies **outside** the country and won.

Earl was an Air Force veteran of that
struggle we know as WWII.

The Great Generation faced the cultural,
political,
social upheavals
of the 1960's …and **won**.

Men and women of the Great Generation were stripped of selfishness
and
self- importance
and were schooled in self discipline,
self sacrifice,
humility,
patriotism,
civic responsibility,
courage in adversity
by the challenges forced upon them.

Members of the Great Generation became the very models of good
husbands and wives,

                                                          good
                                            soldiers in war,
                                                          good
                                            supervisors in
                                            industry.

And yes, the Great Generation made
                              good golfers,
                                    bowlers,
                              good and loyal friends.

They could be counted on for fair and honest work
                                                  and
                                            fair and honest play.

                              And Earl
                              was a full member and
                              worthy member of the
                              Great Generation.

But now the final round of golf is on the card,

                              the last frame has been rolled,
                              the last session
                              with the Koffee Klutch friends at Fayze's
                              is a memory.

Now has come and gone the moment
when a decision had to be made to
save the mobility in a very active man's
hands and feet.

The members of the Great Generation knew risks
and faced crisis –
They also knew
that victory was not inevitable but they
had the courage to face grave
challenges of uncertain outcome.

Earl fought bravely this past week.

> But victory was
> not to be in this battle.

Finally death claimed its prize –
a body of 87 years
> and
> the days among us for Earl Gees
> were finished.

All this would be impossibly sad if this really
were the total and final end.

Into this dark and somber scene we must
flash the brilliant light which is revealed in
one word – **"JESUS"**
> Jesus means "God saves."

> Jesus is the light our faith demands
> we shine on this moment.

And in this light we can see
the day Earl's parents took him to the
parish church for Baptism:

> "Are you unaware that we who were baptized
> into Christ Jesus were baptized into His death
> > so that
> > just as Christ was raised from the
> > dead we too might live in the
> > newness of life."

In the light Jesus shines on this moment we
can see the times Earl approached the
Lord asking for mercy as he confessed his
sins.

In the light Jesus shines on the face of the
dead person
> we can see and remember Earl
> approaching the Lord in Holy Communion.

The Lord who said "If you
eat My body and drink My blood
you have eternal life in you."

In the brilliant light of the resurrected Lord the
sadness of death is revealed as a necessary step to the
total fulfillment of **human life** which can
only be known in the Church of Heaven.

The full and good partner in the Great Generation,
        your devoted dad,
        your dear husband,
        your grandfather,
        your friend, now knows, we can hope, the total
        and lasting greatness of those reborn in baptism,
        claimed as God's portion in this world
                    and
        destined for eternal greatness in the church
        of Heaven.

This is our faith.
This is our consolation.
This is our peace on the day of funeral of Earl Gees.

Resurrection: Our Hope

So what difference does it make?

What **real difference** does an ancient event make? What reason to get

excited about an empty tomb?

What difference does it make or
                    as a smart-aleck type might say of the
            resurrection, of an empty tomb?

                    So what?

        It may seem irreverent to ask that this Easter morning.

                                So what?

Well, what difference it makes is easy for me.

Since last Easter, in one period of 28 days I spent dozens of
hours standing at the bedside of two dying persons.

Their lives had been rich and full.

        They had taught their large family to appreciate the
        Catholic faith.

                Easter was always a very special time in
                    their house

                        because it was the end of a very special
                        season.
Lent was observed with vigor and rigor.
        The whole family absolutely knew it was Lent,
                Penances,

prayers - nightly rosary, kneeling on the linoleum floor,
extra time in Church,

less entertainment,
                all this was
                real stuff lived
                by all in the
                house.

After all that, Easter was an explosion of
relief and joy. Lent was finished,
Easter brought the Easter bunny, candy and spring.

But in the last year
                those two people came to the time when
                they were finishing their journey.
                They were old now - their life chores were
                                finished.

They had **lived well** and only one thing was left,
                they had to **die well.**

Now how can one die well if this
wonderful creation called the human person,
                a creation of so much dignity God Himself
                said of it,

                      "We will make the human person
                      according to our image."

A creation so special that God Himself came by
one day to take on human nature - born of a
human mother,
                born into a carpenter's home and
                life style.
A creation so special, the human person is, that
God died on the cross one day
so that the human person could not only live well
but even much better -
                so that the human person could die
                well. And the human person

can not die well if nothing awaits
that person beyond

the last gasp of breath- the last
beat of the heart.

When all is said and done, nothing we do, will ever even
approach
the importance of dying well.

And the **only way we can die well is** to die
possessed and wrapped in,
secure in,
rejoicing in,
the new life
of the Resurrected Lord.

When one stands at the bedside of dying parents and
when one knows that those parents lived full and
sincere lives of faith
going to church each Sunday,
going to confession regularly,
going to Mass
and receiving Holy Communion several times a week.

Then one knows the importance of Easter
Sunday,
the importance of the Resurrection.
When one stands near the bed of a dying mother
and
dad
and all 11 of their children are singing the songs
of the Christian faith,
praying the prayers of their Catholic
heritage,
then one does not need to ask of the
Resurrection.
So what?
If one can stand with brothers and sisters, with the coffin
of mother about to be lowered into the ground next to her
partner of 67 years

who had been in his final resting place for exactly
28 days,

if one can stand there and find enough composure in
everyone to sing a hymn in honor of Mary, one of those
who went early in the morning on the first day of the
week, while it was still dark and saw the stone removed
from the tomb.

Well, if you can sing such a
song at such a time you need
not ask of Easter and the Resurrection.

So what? What difference does it make?

It makes all the difference. All the
difference.

It allows believers to die well.
For death becomes the gentle door way to the new
life waiting to burst into glorious fulfillment in
heaven.

It allows the survivor the wondrous
comfort of hope

and
peace.

The Resurrection of Jesus simply makes all the difference.
It truly rolls the stone away
from the grave of hopelessness, sadness, despair,
emptiness, loneliness.
The resurrection helps us all to die well and that's truly
most important in life.

And dying well happens most especially to those who
have tried to live well.

And those who try to live well are those who take the advice of
Saint Paul in the first reading:

"Brothers and sisters, seek what is above, where Christ is seated at the right hand of God.
Think of what is above, not of what is on earth. For you have died, and your life is
hidden with Christ in God. When Christ your life appears, then you too will appear with Him in glory."

Take that advice this Easter
day and you will not only live
well but more importantly one
day, die well.

What difference does Easter make?

Simple! It makes an eternal difference.

Catechists Guard Our Faith

Around the Diocese and around the nation today it
is <u>Catechetical Sunday.</u>

That may not be the opening sentence to get
your most rapt attention.
It doesn't sound <u>too</u> exciting - Catechetical Sunday.

The word itself - what does it mean?

And
if I know the meaning <u>does</u> it
make any difference and <u>should it</u>
make any difference to me or
anybody?

The word **"catechetics"** comes from the Greek word
"catecheo"
and that word <u>means</u> to echo

or

<u>resound</u>

or

sound again

a message given to the catechist.

The catechist has no message which
is **original**
or
which is her or his very own invention

or

insight.

The catechist sounds again

or

echos
a message <u>given</u> to him or her.

For the Catholic Catechist that is the message
derived from Christ and the teaching Church.

The catechist **guards** a message, doesn't **create** a
message.

When Pope John Paul II published the **Catechism of
the Catholic Church he wrote these words**:

>"**Guarding the deposit** of faith is the **mission**
>which the Lord entrusted to His Church and
>which she fulfills in every age."

>God sent His own **Son as a teacher** of the
>divine truths which are the flaming
>heart of the deposit of faith.

The Sacred Scripture tells us Jesus went about **teaching**.

>But the day came when His life
>among us was finished.

Saint Matthew concludes his gospel
with the words of Jesus to the Apostles.

"Full authority has been given to Me,
 Both in heaven and on earth---
>go therefore and make disciples of all nations.

>Baptize them in the name of the Father
>>the Son

>>>and
>>>The Holy Spirit.

>**Teach them** to carry out **everything**
>I have commanded you."

Teach them everything I have taught you
>>sound again
>>re-sound
>>echo the message
>>I have given you.

Jesus says **"Gentlemen - you are catechists"**
>Echo what I told you.

147

So long as the full teaching of **Jesus'** message
Continued, the Church remained **one.**

But then some began to sound
a new message
                adding things
                subtracting things

                        and from that day 400 years ago
                        and continuing to this very moment we got a
great splitting and re-splitting
                        of the family of Christ.

The role of the catechist is extremely important.
The unity of the Church depends on good, holy, humble catechists.
 It takes **HOLINESS OF LIFE**, humility, to be a
servant to the old, but ever new message
Christ gave us.

Humility - what a wondrous way Christ teaches
that virtue in the Gospel today.

            He sets a child in the midst of His
            squabbling apostles
                    squabbling over who is best
                            who is greatest
                            who is closest to the
                            boss, the center of power.

            And Jesus says
                    "The greatest among you is
                    The one who serves the rest."

And then He sets a child at the center of
the scene, puts His arms around the little
one and says
            "Whoever receives one such child
            as this in My name receives Me."

The Catechist mostly spends time with the little ones.
The Catechist is **servant** to the little ones
                        to the little ones' parents
                and most especially **servant to the Lord** for the

Catechist can only
echo,
re-sound
the message
Christ gave us.

What a strange world we live in that
catechists who re-sound Christ's
message are criticized as outdated.

The catechist is necessarily a humble person - no
other mind,
no other spirit   will allow the catechist to do the job well.
The job of catechist is extremely challenging. Other messages, other
teachers call out to every child, every soul.
So many of the messages are contrary to the message the good God
gave us **through Jesus**.

So many messages are contrary to the **good**
message of the **Ten** Commandments.

So many messages proclaim a **creed** that is totally of this world.

I believe I **must** be #1
I believe I must have this or that material thing.
I believe I must do my thing
I believe I must be popular
I believe I will decide for myself what is right and wrong
I believe I must throw all my time into my career, no matter the effect
on my marriage.
I believe homosexual action, contraception, abortion are
fully acceptable.

The great messages of our secular world
put the "I" absolutely first.

A message is taught
over and again by the world to our children and to all
which is exactly opposite
Of the message of Jesus in the Gospel today.

How desperately we need our Catholic **School** Catechists and
our **Wednesday night religious education Catechists**.

They are **front line** soldiers
 in the battle for your child's soul and your soul.

The Church and western
civilization have slipped into
a period of decline from which neither will recover until the
Eternal Truths are re-echoed
and re-appropriated by Church and society.
It is a bitter pill for a self-important
world to swallow but...

The greatest among you is
the one who serves the need of all to hear again the Eternal Truths.
It is not an easy message nor an easy job,
but it is the message of Christ and therefore it is the
message the catechist must echo and
                              resound
                    echo
                         and
                         resound, again.

Pray for all those who are **catechists**
to our children.

Pray for their parents.

Pray for the children and young people
that the words of divine truth,
          the lives of the saints,
          the beauty of the commandments,
          the love of the church,
          the power of the sacraments,
                    may light a fire in
                    the tender spirits of the young and
                    grow steadily stronger for their good,
                              the good of the family,
                              the good of the Church,
                    the good of the country,
                              and
                         the glory of God.

Funeral of James Pearce

First of all this morning I extend sympathy
and consolation on behalf of Blessed Sacrament Parish
and my own behalf to the three sons

James,
John
Thomas,
to the grandchildren,
Elizabeth,
Emily,
and
John,
to brother George.

SONS, you have special blood in your veins.
GRANDCHILDREN, you have been deeply blessed in
         your grandfather.

Brother George, know the world is better for the
         one you were privileged to call "brother",
         your closest brother, your vacationing companion.
But to you JEANETTE, we turn with special
tenderness this somber morning.

Your wonderfully gifted,
    wonderfully educated,
    wonderfully generous and faithful husband
    has completed the course of his years.

How difficult it must be to sit in that spot
only a few steps removed from where
a strong,

handsome,
smiling,
athletic guy stood on December 27, 1951.
A brief break in military service allowed him
to stand there waiting for a beautiful young bride
to make her way down this long aisle.

You delivered
        your hopes and dreams,
        your soul and body to your Jim that day, Jeanette
           and
        he gave himself totally to you and
        what adventures were awaiting the two of you.

A man for whom the WORLD became his NEIGHBORHOOD
was extraordinarily dependent
on one who would faithfully keep the home fires burning

with a MOTHER'S CARE AND LOVE, to GUIDE AND
CIVILIZE his sons.
A man of piercing intellectual power was especially
dependent on one who would and could love him,
without reservation, as he immersed himself in his
work--a man passionately, stubbornly, driven to succeed.

A man who went about a professional life
leaving his mark on the electrical engineering
world, in truly extra ordinary fashion, was
wonderfully appreciative of one who would
                listen to his dreams,
                appreciate his fears,
                and bake a good pie.

A man who was a champion, real and true
in so many fields,
      Was it high school debating - he was champion.
      Was it baseball - he was champion.
      Was it the mysteries of electronics,
                circuit breakers,
                automatic control systems -
                he was a champion.

Was it teaching and
        inspiring his sons,
        providing for his family,
        sharing his talents with other fathers' sons in the
            scouting or explorer post -
        he was a champion.

Was it lecturing and teaching exotic engineering procedures
at the university of,
        Brussels,

        Beijing,

        Geneva,

        Madrid,

        Nice,

        Sidney.
Was it writing learned articles,
was it the genius of invention,
was it driving learned lawyers to
        fits of frustration in court room battles
                            defending his
                            company against
                            liability claims
                                or
                            patent infringement -

HE WAS A CHAMPION.

BUT JIM, THE CHAMPION, HAS FALLEN.

THE CHAMPION'S TROPHIES AND HONORS HAVE ALL BEEN
EARNED AND COLLECTED - IT IS NOW THE TIME
TO PRAISE A GREAT MAN.

A famous person was asked: "What do you think of life?"

"I think," the man said, "it's a
PREDICAMENT which PRECEDES death."

Jim has navigated the predicament well and now he has come ,
we pray, to the total fulfillment of human life,
to safe harbor at the feet of the Shepherd and Savior, Jesus,
the Lord. The final light, we pray, has flashed
through the darkness of death marking
the beginning of eternity for Jim.

The Fall of the year is a great Christian preacher.
The first morning after Jim's death was white with the first heavy
freeze of the season. It reminds us that
      all things bright and beautiful,
    all things intelligent or merely animate,
      all living things are born to die.

October 4th, in the year 1226 a man, who changed the world
of his day, died.

Saint Francis of Assisi was that man.

The Church celebrates his life and death each year on this day,
October 4th.

When he felt his end was near the "little poor man", "Poverello" ,
as Francis was known,
asked that the Gospel of Saint John be read, beginning where it says:

    "Now before the feast of the Passover, Jesus
    knew that His hour had come to pass from
    this world to the Father, having loved His own
    who were in the world, and He loved them to the end."

And Francis listened as the betrayal
of Jesus was recounted.

He listened as Jesus was condemned to death.

He heard the pounding of nails through the sacred flesh.

In his faith-filled soul he saw the place of burial.

He heard the words of the angel spoken to the weeping
Mary Magdalene as she stood by the tomb:

"Then the angel said: Woman why are you weeping. He is
                    risen, He is not here."

When the long reading was finished,
fortified with the
re-assuring
wonder of God's power
over death,
Francis said: "Welcome, my Sister Death" - and soon
                                   he
                                       died.
On this October 4th when we gather in respect
and in sadness for a truly remarkable life,
now finished in its course, we must put this special life and special man
in the most special light.

That special light is the light shed ON AND IN Jim
by the gift the Crucified and Risen One gave him
on the day of his baptism.

        "Do you not know that we who were baptized
        into Christ Jesus were baptized into His death, so
        that just as He rose to new life so might we
        too live a new life."

By reason of Jim's work many walks and stairs,
roads and paths are brilliantly and safely lighted, leading
people safely home after work or play.

One path and one home is important beyond all
others.
                It is a narrow path and challenging
                and it leads to our eternal
                home.

The human soul was made for God
and it will not rest until it rests in Him.
The path is brightly lighted for those who walk
in the light which is Christ.

"I am the light of the world, come
follow Me and I will lead you home to the Father."

In his last months I visited a good deal with Jim.

We talked of his life, his work, his family,
his illness.

We talked of death.
Jim did not go
easily into the gathering
gloom.

He was a competitor, willing if necessary,
to do hand-to-hand combat with sickness and death.
Five days before he died the two of us sat outside on a warm evening
watching the light of the setting sun paint the bluffs
a beautiful amber color.

Jim felt something beyond the sunset that Saturday night.

He said "Father, it's BEEN a good life."

It was as though
this special man
had surveyed the
YEARS AND ACCOMPLISHMENTS
of life and now was
saying, WELCOME, MY SISTER DEATH.

Permit me to tell you what I THOUGHT but did not
say to his remark: "It's been a good life."

My thought was: "Jim, you haven't seen anything yet."

I remembered St. Paul's words: "The mind of man cannot
imagine what God has prepared
for those who love Him."

In the months in which I saw Jim weekly for
Holy Communion, after
we finished our short ritual of Communion
for the sick, he invariably said,

        "Thanks, I needed that."

Yes, Jim, you needed that Precious Gift
shot through with Divine Power and Divine Love.

You needed it Jim, WE ALL NEED THAT
Bread which has come down from heaven

        which if you eat it, Jesus said,
        YOU HAVE ETERNAL LIFE IN YOU.

You have eternal life in you - Jim may have
had his reservations about the Church at a
        moment of his life - so... we all do - the wonder
        is too great not to question, not
        to argue,
        but in the moment of his illness Jim
        said as Christ said in the Garden before
        His death:

        "FATHER TAKE THIS CUP OF SUFFERING FROM ME,
        BUT NOT MY WILL, BUT YOURS BE DONE."

Jim had come to that place in the spiritual life - a
very good place indeed -- let God's will be done.
        That lived faith,
         that resignation to God's will,
         that eager reception of Holy Communion,
         that promise of Christ at Baptism,
         the promise
      of eternal life,
           all these and more are
              our consolation,
              our hope,
              our peace,
              on the day of funeral
                for
              James N. Pearce.

Archbishop Burke

Last Monday I was among those who sat below the great ambo
in St. Louis Cathedral in that city.

The huge church was filled with 1800 people.

Archbishop Burke looked down from that
speaking place, 12-15 feet above the crowd.

The Bishop we have known so well,
the farm boy from Richland Center and Stratford spoke so powerfully.

Over and over again the great crowd broke into his
talk with applause.
>It seemed the more strong the statement,
>the louder the applause.

>So when he spoke of the
>**dignity of life**
>from conception to natural death,
>the applause was loudest and longest.

And why does the Archbishop and the
Church make so much of that simple issue?
Because of words such as the first reading:

>"Before I formed you in the womb I knew you.
>Before you were born I dedicated you,
>a prophet to the nations, I appointed you.

>Stand up and tell them
>all that I command you.

Be not crushed on their account.
For it is I, this day, who has
made you a fortified city,
a wall of brass,
a pillar of iron
against the whole land."

The strong and confident Archbishop
also had a **softer and very moving**
part of his speech.

"We must draw near to the
Sacred Heart of Jesus.

We must draw strength from that
immense love poured out for us.

We must **find joy** in that heart
pierced for us and for our salvation.

The opening of that heart
of Jesus with a spear was
also the opening of heaven for
all who would put their heart in
the heart of Christ.

Look into that face of Jesus -
see there the caring of the
eternal God for you.

Look into the **eyes** that hold you in
their gaze and
know that no matter the sin
in our life those eyes hold you
in their gaze because Christ wants
you to accept His love and
His saving mercy.

Look into that **face** and
see the face of mercy.
fall on your knees in adoration

159

before the Lord
present in the tabernacle,
present in the appearance of bread.
The good Archbishop called everyone
there to a life of holiness...
bring your needs to Him,
bring your worries,
bring your sadness,
bring your fear,
bring your fatigue,
bring your illness,
bring your family,
bring your spouse,
bring your children,
bring your marriage,
bring everything of you
to the Lord in the Blessed Sacrament.

**He is really as present there as He was to
the people in the Gospel.**

Today is the end of "Catholic Schools" week.
Our Catholic schools effort, in time and money is
wasted if we get through school without developing
a great love for the Name and the Person of Jesus
and
an equally great love for the name and the glory
of the Church
He founded, our
Catholic Church.

In the great Cathedral of St. Louis,
the new Archbishop was applauded repeatedly
through his speech.

It was like the Gospel reading this morning.

All spoke highly of Jesus and were
amazed at the wonderful words which
came from His mouth.

"Ah, what a wonderful speaker.", they said of Jesus.
"What powerful words.", they said of Jesus.
"What a joy that He comes to our synagogue.", they said of Jesus
" What an honor to our
city that this Jesus is so wise,
so intelligent,
so handsome,
so good.",
they said of Jesus.
And how long did that last?

In the space of an hour they were ready to
throw Him over the cliff at the edge of town.

What happened?
Jesus told the people He was the Messiah. They had to change
their ways drastically to be as good as
even the pagans that lived in the neighboring countries.

Our **Catholic faith and education is empty of power** if we want a
Jesus who does not challenge us to live a new life, a life in Him,
live the life He gave us in baptism.
Do we accept Jesus as King and prophet?

The shepherd King of our souls and lives
The Son of God and Son of Mary born in a barn,
The Son of God and Son of Mary,
scourged,
crowned with thorns,
crucified,
pierced with a lance,
who came as a Divine **Teacher**.

We accept Him as King of our souls and lives
when we give 90 minutes of our time each weekend for Mass
when we tithe, 10% of our income for charity.
when we totally accept and keep God's moral law of sex within
marriage.
Total acceptance of the right to life
and dignity and sacredness of life from conception to
natural death.

Do we accept Jesus in every and all aspects
of life--- the good days
               the not so good days?
Does our Catholic education effort move us to
look at Jesus with love
and move us to pursue the call to holiness,
our call to be
disciples truly and fully?

Or do we hear and then
               do we try to hurl Him over the cliff
               because He is a disturbance to the peace
          which we have reached with the world and
          its ways by compromising Christ's
          teaching
               and
               accepting the politically acceptable
          ways of the world.

Our **past** was filled with Christ's presence
or we wouldn't be here this morning.

Our **present** is filled with Christ's presence as we
          listen to His Word,
          receive His total Self in Holy Communion
          and realize we are brothers and sisters in
          the Lord so we find Christ in others.

Our faith-filled **future** is dependent on God's grace
          for the success of our schools
          and the choice of each of us to accept Christ totally
now and thus protect the Church of Christ into the future.

Vocations Come With Prayer

Several times during the church year the
image of the Good Shepherd is put out before us.

This image is a reminder that Christ is the **first
Shepherd of the Church.**

What a joy to know He **is** the first shepherd
　　　　　　　the first pastor,
　　　　　　　　　the first priest, **to the parish**.

The visible priests
the visible pastor

　　　　　　　　are only co-operators
　　　　　　　　　　　or
　　　　　　　　living instruments through
　　　　　　　　which Christ the pastor,
　　　　　　　　　　Christ the priest,
　　　　　　　　　　Christ the shepherd,
　　　　　　　　watches over Blessed Sacrament parish
　　　　　　　　and every other parish in the universal church.

Good Shepherd Sunday has become for
several decades now a spiritual day of prayer
for **vocations to the priesthood and consecrated life.**

On this Good Shepherd Sunday
the Gospel has a phrase which has special meaning
to me.

**"I give them eternal life and they shall
never perish."** Let me explain.

Its about 15 months now that I stood

by the bedside of my dying parents.

                    Both gone in the space of 28 days.
          As I looked at their faces each in
          their turn growing more ashen,
                   more collapsed,

I remembered so many days in Church when they
       were healthy, strong
and
well dressed as they always were when they came
       to church.

I was there at the head of the aisle
       when they came for Communion -

          I would say to Mother and to Dad

          "The Body of Christ"

That precious Body of Christ which is the source of
eternal life and I, their son, could give it
 to them.

I can most honestly tell you
that I frequently thought of the
wonder and the joy of that moment when Mother
       and Dad grew older and their steps less vigorous

and, as each lay dying I most clearly reflected on
the words of the gospel today

"I give them eternal life and they shall never perish."

That is not arrogance,
          nor overpowering pride

that is humble recognition of the beauty of the
priesthood
        and the glory of the Holy Eucharist.

And it is all privilege of the one called to be
priest.

Without the priesthood the Eucharist
and
The Church
would simply cease to exist.
Without the priesthood no one can correctly
and truthfully offer a bit of bread to a
communicant and say
"The Body of Christ"
"The Body of Christ"

Vocations to the priesthood are
nurtured in prayer,
answered in prayer,
and
preserved in prayer.

We remember Jesus spent 3 years in His
public life.

Those were the most important three years
in the history of the world.

Three years of 33
and
where do we find Jesus repeatedly in
those 3 years.

Alone in the wilderness
on the mountainside
at the lakeshore.

Alone - praying,
praying,
praying.

Here we have the Son of God who changed water into wine,
raised the dead to life,
simply by speaking a word.

Here He is repeatedly praying because He had
a job to do of which the human Christ felt the
need of His Father's help.

The Sacred Scriptures say Christ
spent the night in prayer
       and
then went and picked His 12
special Apostles from among the larger
group of followers.

    Christ prayed for vocations. - Then he went to call
                     and
                most especially <u>men</u> answered.

In our day we say we have a shortage
of vocations. Is this loss of faith on our part?
      Is that blasphemy?
      Is that to say God has forgotten His people?

We remember Sacred Scripture says:

"If a mother should forget her child I will not
forget you."

"I have written you on the palm of my hand."

But prayer is still so important.

Prayer takes us to the heart of God.
Prayer is reaching out to the Father's love
and compassion.

      Prayer is our response to Christ's invitation.

Seek and you will find,
Knock and it will be opened,
Ask and it will be given to you.

Let us always pray that those God is calling will respond
to the call.

And if you are one who has suffering in
your life
      family or marriage problems
      loss of a life partner or loved one

166

offer that suffering to God - we must
always remember Jesus didn't save the
world by changing water into wine
> or
>> feeding the 5000 with a couple loves
>> of bread

but by freely offering His suffering to
His Father.

To freely offer your suffering to the Lord
is a most powerful thing.

Finally the Mass is the center of all prayer
most especially prayer for vocations.

In the sacrament of the altar vocations to the
priesthood and the consecrated life are discovered.

> Here vocations are born
>> and
> here they are strengthened.

This is why anyone truly interested in
vocations to the priesthood and consecrated life
spends time before
the Blessed Sacrament

> and why parishes which have regular
> Eucharistic Adoration have more young
> men and women answering the call to priesthood
>> and consecrated life.

My dream is that we could have many
more hours of Eucharistic Adoration each week.

It is the school of holiness and Christ Himself is the
Teacher. It is the source of vocations.

It is here, before the Blessed Sacrament
that we are moved to say with
Saint Peter,
> "Lord, it is good to be here."

Our Church:
Christ Present Here and Now

On Thursday morning I was one of those who
stood in the pouring rain,

> fierce flashes of lightening,
> booming blasts of thunder, for well over an hour.

The **ground breaking** for the Shrine Church of Our Lady of
Guadalupe was memorable for many reasons.

As I surveyed the huddled, rain-soaked crowd
last Thursday morning a wonderful vision
came to mind:

> I saw:
> - the **beauty** of the **Church**!
> - the beauty of a **faith-filled crowd**!
> - the beauty of a brave and good **bishop!**
> - the beauty of a **life** on earth lived with

> a vision of things and persons beyond
> this earth which makes standing
> in lightening and thunder acceptable,
> and sloshing through mud and running water
> a work of **love** and an act of **faith**.

I surveyed that crowd of rich and poor

> dignitaries and common folk

> and I saw the **beauty** of the **Church,**

> crowned head and day laborer
> standing in mud and rain to bring

honor to two who stand over all;

Christ and **His Holy Mother**.
The crowd said by their presence - for the happy task for which
we gather there is no inconvenience great enough to
keep us away.

In the thunder and rain I saw the **beauty of the people of God,**
the **Church**, willing to spend **great chunks** of **time**
and great **amounts of treasure** on a
shrine dedicated to the Mother of God.

I saw **the beauty of the Church** in that rain soaked scene.

> The **beauty of a Church** which has spoken
> with clarity and infallible truth of the
> things of God since the day our Divine
> Lord Said:
>
> "Father, they are your
>   gift to Me" in the gospel today.

I saw in that wet and muddy scene the **beauty of a Church**
literally and **truly** let **down from heaven**.

As we remember from last Sunday's readings:
"I saw the holy city, the church
coming down from heaven from God as beautiful as a bride prepared
for her husband."

> The beauty of a church not
> **invented** by **man** but **RECEIVED**
> from God .

The beauty of a people **taught by** God.

> In our day we have many people
> who presume to **teach** the Church rather
> than accept the teaching from the Church.

I submit that those who would teach the Church

have created 30 - 35, 000 protestant churches in our
country alone.
I saw the **beauty of a Church taught by God** when I listened to the
words of the Bishop.

There is so much **beauty** and **truth** and **love** and **grace** to be seen in
the church on a rain soaked, muddy day on
a hillside because

> Christ and the Church are **one**, and Christ is
> > All **beauty,**
> > All **truth,**
> > All **love,**
> > All **goodness**.

Saint Joan of Arc questioned by Doctors of Law,
> Doctors of Theology
was asked tricky questions about Christ and the Church.

And as quoted in the Catholic Catechism,
the uneducated peasant girl said:

> "All I can say is that Christ and the
> Church are one and the same."
That line sounds very much
> like Pope Leo the Great who said,

"Everything that was in Christ has passed over into
the Church."

Consider - all of us know people who don't go to mass
at all or only when it is a slow day in their social
calendar.

But if I could promise Jesus of Nazareth was going to
be here, in the flesh and blood, the walls
would not hold the crowd I'm certain.

Well, what **CAN** I promise? Jesus of Nazareth
in the flesh and blood is present because everything that was
in Christ has passed over into the Church.

The beauty of the Church is totally beyond human making
                                        and
                                        human understanding.

The beauty and dignity of the Church is cemented
forever in the words of Jesus in the Gospel today
where we read :
                "Lifting His eyes to heaven, Jesus prayed,

                saying

                Holy Father, I pray not only for them
                but also for those who will believe in Me
                through their word."

On a rain soaked hillside or in this dry Church we
do the acts of **faith** and **prayer** and **worship** and this is
part of the **beauty** of the Church but even more
spectacular beauty is that the **Son of God prays for us.**

The Holy Spirit:
Our Power Source

Today we celebrate the moment God solved the
power shortage in the Church.

Today we celebrate the day God **energized**
a few dispirited men with a new spirit---
                    The Holy Spirit.
            The Holy Spirit made them new men.
Today we celebrate the moment when
Christ caste fire on the earth and
                    we celebrate the day that fire
                    began to spread,
                            as the first reading tells
                            us today.

Today we celebrate the coming of the Spirit of Truth
of Whom Jesus said He will teach you all things.

                            Jesus had **promised** that Spirit
                            and today we celebrate the
                            delivery of the
                            promise.

The Holy Spirit is the **power source**
for the Church's life.

It is because of the Holy Spirit that the crowds were amazed and in
wonder at what these fishermen,
tax collectors
and grapevine tenders were doing on Pentecost day.

It was with the power of the Holy Spirit that
they spoke in languages everyone understood.
 It must have been an exhilarating experience for the
Apostles that day when they proclaimed God's truth about
Jesus - His death and Resurrection and Ascension.

> It would not **always be exhilarating** –
> The day would soon come when the crowds would turn
> against them as the crowds had turned against Jesus.

Later, it would be with the power of the Holy Spirit
that **Peter** cured a **beggar** at the temple steps.
The power of the Holy Spirit was the reason
the **shadow** of Peter **falling** on the sick was
enough to effect a cure as the Bible tells us.

It was the power of the **Holy Spirit** working when
Paul healed the man who had fallen from a third
story window who had been listening to Paul preach.

It was the power of the Holy Spirit
which provided the courage for these early
Christians to speak God's truth into
an unbelieving and hostile world.

The power of the Holy Spirit
has encouraged and consoled an army of martyrs
through the centuries and
strengthens bishops and priests and lay people to speak with power and
conviction
to those who do not respect life from conception to natural death.

Let us not be romantic about this Pentecost Day.

It was very costly to the Apostles then
and to us now, in purely human terms.

It would not be long before the **Apostle James,**
first Bishop of Jerusalem, would be
put to death for preaching and teaching the
truth and the message of the **life,**
> **death and**
> **Resurrection** of Jesus

To proclaim the truth of Christ is both the
privilege and burden of the Church.

Jesus proclaimed the Truth about
God and claimed to be the Truth about God ---it gained **Him** a **CROSS!**
The Apostles went out preaching the Truth Christ
proclaimed -
>It got all the Apostles, save one, a
>violent, martyr's death.

Nothing is so demanding as the challenge to accept
God's truth and fashion our lives according to it.

At the present moment from the East coast to
the West coast and in between
>Catholic bishops are asking Catholic
>politicians to do some serious thinking
>about themselves as Catholics and the
>decisions they make.

One bishop had a $100,000 pledge to a church project recalled because
he spoke too strongly to pro-choice and pro-abortion politicians. His
response : "The church was born in the poverty of the stable and the
cross and if it must be poor for teaching God's truth, so be it."

The cry goes up that the bishops are meddling
in politics, then why do politicians meddle in the Church?

>That is exactly what was said of Christ in the
>moment of His passion and death.

>That is what was said of Peter,
>>James,
>>John.

That is exactly what was said of every
martyr and confessor who ever turned the light
of God's Truth on the darkness of a purely secular way of thinking.

The Church is under attack for the **right reasons.**

>There is **nobility and dignity** in that position.

When our beloved Church enriched with the treasury of
God's eternal
      and
      God's revealed Truth
                 is perfectly at peace with
                 a non-believing world then
                 we as Church
                 have much to worry about.

The Infant Jesus was the finest and richest gift of the
Holy Spirit.
                The Infant Jesus
                represented a great and immediate
                threat to secular power and quickly
                        blood flowed
                and very interestingly
                it was the blood of
                infants which stained the earth.

The church in our day is no longer the infant Jesus
but the adult Jesus and the adult Church
enriched with God's Truth by the Holy Spirit
              about the world
              about life and death
              about human kind.

When the Church, that's you and me who live this life seriously,
when the church is not misunderstood and persecuted,
as Christ promised would happen then we must ask:
                    "Have we abandoned the
                    truths the Holy Spirit
                    has given us?"

 A wonderful lady remarked this week that
she perceived a wave of orthodoxy;
              a wave of new courage,

                  sweeping the country in
proclaiming God's Truth into a world that hates God's truth.

The words and actions of bishops,
                              priests,
                              lay people,
                across the land indicate it is so.

It is exhilarating to respond to God's truth.
It is redeeming.
It is our nobility,
      our dignity and
it is our privilege to be witnesses to God's Truth and
the Holy Spirit will strengthen us for the task.

Since Pentecost there is no power shortage in
the Church - let us plug into
                        and
                illuminate the world with that power.

The Law Of The Gift

On this Labor Day Weekend the liturgy
gives us a parable of man planning to
construct a tower and a king marching into battle.

Two kinds of labor.

Our world is filled with an enormous number of
professions,
careers,
jobs.

> All manner of labor, of mind or body, or
> both by which one can earn a living.

I propose to you today one labor most significant
and most necessary.

The one work we must all accomplish if we hope
to know our full dignity and fulfillment
as human persons.

> The labor we must accomplish
> is the labor of choosing to
> work at being the disciple of the
> Lord.

It's a radical choice and a difficult choice.

Jesus says today,

"If anyone comes to Me
without hating his father and mother,
brothers and sisters,
even his own life
He cannot be My disciple."

Jesus demands our total self... a radical choice.

Jesus asks us to live the **law of the gift.**

The law of the gift!   What is that?

John Paul II has made that phrase popular.

The law of the gift.

The law of the gift says that
it is absolutely built into nature
that we will be fulfilled, or perfected, or satisfied

as human persons **only** when we make a gift of ourselves to others...

radically and totally in marriage, in priesthood, in single life,

that is the law of the gift.

We find fulfillment in making ourselves a gift to others.

And so Jesus in the gospel says you must
love Me more than father or mother...
radical , total gift of self to Christ.

In Jesus is our total perfection and fulfillment as human beings so,

the law of the gift says
that if I give myself totally to
Jesus I have lost nothing
                but
                gained everything

178

because, in Christ is every human joy
and perfection.

On this Labor Day weekend I suggest that the most noble,
fulfilling,
enduring,
uplifting
work most people can possibly do, involves the **work** of building
happy marriages and families.
Happy marriages give us
happy children
and
happy children give us
happy schools,
happy communities, nations
and happy children
will likely someday
build **their** happy family.

The work of nurturing marriage and family is a labor of love
and that means it is a
labor of self-giving... the law of the gift.

It can be very difficult. After all, the way Christ won
His bride the Church was by death on the cross.

He gave himself totally and died doing it but,
He came to a new life because
He gave himself totally.

His life was the perfection of
the law of the gift.
New life and fulfillment came from self-giving.

So, in the labor of love called marriage and family
the law of the gift
says only in making one's self a total gift
to one's spouse will one be fulfilled in marriage.

The person who would keep
one foot in the **single life**
and one foot in the married life
can never be totally fulfilled in

marriage because one is not living correctly.

The **law of the gift** applies, as well, to
parent and child, child and parent.
Children will learn the law of the gift from a
mother and dad who have clearly given themselves
as gift to their partners and it is evident in the
>
words,
>
gestures,
>
actions,
>
smiles that pass between them.

Young children, when very young, are very cute and
naturally, very selfish... That's just the way infants and
the very young are.
Those children will grow up cute and generous,
unselfish kids who find joy and fulfillment
in helping others
>
if they learn the law of the gift
from parents who live that law.
If they don't learn it from
seeing it in action they'll probably
never learn it!!

This Labor Day I suggest to you... No labor of any kind,
no matter how humble or how exalted

is in the same ballpark with the dignity and importance

of working at a happy marriage and a happy family.

To fulfill that labor successfully there is
no greater help than to approach the One Who says,

"This is My body,

My blood,

My everything, for you."

180

Christ lived the **LAW OF THE GIFT** totally.

Christ is our model and our inspiration,

and

our strength.

Seth Hammes Funeral

I begin this somber morning by extending words of
sympathy to Erica
              and
              Rachel,
        maternal grandmother, Janet Rentmeester,
        paternal grandparents, Dave and Betty Hammes
            all the uncles and aunts,
                    cousins,
      to Seth's classmates, friends, and teachers,

and most especially to parents
                          Steven and Patrice.

        Steve, the one who you saw passing on the
        family name will **not**.

                Patrice, you brought forth Seth into
                the world in **physical** pain and suffering

                        you now suffer with **spiritual**
                        and **emotional** pain as your son
                        is born into a new life.

This is a melancholy day in a melancholy season.

It seems like yesterday when the **tulips** were blooming,
                        the **maples** were just budding,
                        the **grass** just greening,
                        the **fawns** of spring were dressed
                        in their white spotted coats,
                        the spring and summer birds were still
                        new visitors.

But already the flower gardens are mature,
> the maple leaves are turning color and soon to fall,
> the fall and winter birds are beginning to
> replace the birds of spring and summer.

In a 4 – 5 month blaze
> of color and energy, the life cycle
> in nature has made one more
> turn.

Today we come to bury one in whom the vital
juices of the **springtime of life**
were still fresh and new.

Mother and Dad,
> grandparents, uncles, aunts, friends,

> you remember clearly the day of his
> birth and baptism into the
> life of Christ.

> His early school years,
> > his developing fascination with computers,
> > fireworks,
> > family celebrations,
> > 4-wheelers,
> > electronics of all kinds,
> > photography,

his **care of** and love **for**
> a dog named "Boomer,"
> all the stuff of the springtime of life.
> Seth lived all his life in the springtime of his life.
> > All was filled with excitement,
> > > energy,
> > > growth in
> > > body,
> > > mind,
> > > spirit,
> > Springtime – the promise of harvest,
> > > of maturity,
> > > the promise of reward
> > > for

labor and career,
the joy of marriage and
family,
all was still stuff of the future.
But then, suddenly, springtime is eternal.

Seth will forever
be remembered only for the springtime
of
his life because there was to be no more.

Today one young life **has finished** its course,

but many lives, young and older will forever be marked
by **the day** they heard of his death.

The day they attended the wake and funeral of
a young son, brother, nephew,
friend, classmate,
who only knew the
springtime of life.

Some may want to ask
where was the good God when this happened?

I can **tell you** where God was on a Saturday afternoon
when Seth saw autumn leaves
through the fading vision of the dying.

God was in the same place he was on the
day **loves embrace** resulted in the beginning
of a new human life that one day
would answer to the name Seth.

God was in the same place on Saturday last
as He was on the day He gifted Seth in
so many ways in the silence of mother's womb.

God was in the same place when Seth stepped
into the woods with his camcorder as He was
on the day Seth stepped across the threshold of
his kindergarten classroom.
If God was in the same place on a day of
tragedy and death as He was on a day **of joy and life,** then we

ask a further question: Why? Why this?

I confess **I do not know,** why this.

But this I do know.

That the mercy of God is not ended.

I do know that God's love is not **withdrawn.**

I do know that the **Lord who wept** at the death
of His friend Lazarus is with us this morning.

I do know that the Lord whose heart was repeatedly moved
with pity when He saw the suffering and struggles,
sadness and pain
of others is with us this morning.

I do know that the Lord whose side was
pierced with a spear as He hung on the
cross is with us as our own hearts are pierced
with the sword of pain and loss.

I do know that the Lord who said,

"Come to Me you who are weary and
heavily burdened and I will refresh you."

is with us now.

Friends, there is
no sure and certain
reference point,
marker,
guidepost,
which is totally of human making.
Only one
is given us who could
say, I am the guide,
I am the light,
I am the truth,
follow Me.
I will be
with you all

days until the
end of the world.

On a day such as today
we turn to Christ. He conquered
death and we turn to
Him for help in
conquering our experience
of Seth's death.

Life is never as precious as when we see how
suddenly it can be shortened,
suddenly it can be ended.

I wish to reach out in word and sympathy to all Seth's classmates and
young friends.

It is a sad and lonely day,
    a day of questions,
    a day of suffering.

This day you bear **the burden of suffering**.

    Suffering can make us angry, bitter, cold
    people, almost as if our hearts shrivel.

Or suffering can make us more loving,
                  compassionate,
                  generous.
      Almost as if our hearts expand.

We do not choose whether or not to suffer.

One of the most painful aspects of suffering
is that we do not choose the time,
              the place,
              the manner
      that suffering comes into our lives.

What we do choose is what we will do with that
suffering.

186

We can choose to allow it to shrivel
                    our hearts and spirits
                         or
          to expand our hearts and spirits.

It would honor the memory of Seth if his death
expanded our hearts and spirits so that all who
knew and loved him would become "gentle giants"
                                   of love,
                                   compassion,
                                   caring.

Steve and Patrice it must seem such a short time
ago when you carried your infant son to the
parish church for Baptism.

               That was the most important
               moment in your son's life. That was the day
               the promise of eternal life was born in Seth.

That is the moment that takes the rawest edge from
your pain this morning.

               In that moment life in its total fullness
               was opened to Seth
                         and
                    whether his life was 17, 67 or 97 years,
                    the day of Baptism into Christ would ever be
                    the turning point.
Saint Paul says:
          "Don't you know that we who were
          baptized into Christ Jesus were baptized into
          His death so that just as Christ was raised
          to new life we too might be raised to
          new life in Him."

So today we mourn but we do not mourn like
those who have no hope.
We **rejoice** in the gift of life which was Seth.

We **mourn** over a gift of life ended so tragically
                              and
                         so soon.

But we rejoice that Seth has been called to the total
fulfillment of human life which is an out-of-this-world
experience.

> Seth's entry into life after death is
> our consolation,
> our joy,
> our peace on the day of funeral.

Little Tabernacles

The angels in heaven are envious of you today,
boys and girls.

The angels do not have a day like you are having.

The angels cannot be a tabernacle for Jesus
because they have no body.

Today you will be the special tabernacle
in which Jesus most especially wants to stay.

Up there is a golden tabernacle.

It is beautiful,
it is precious,
and it holds Jesus.

But down here are little tabernacles

more beautiful
and
more precious
        than that one or any
        other in the whole world.

You are much more beautiful because you were
created in God's own image,
and God is beautiful beyond anything we can imagine.

You are more precious because you are a
child of God,

and one so loved and so precious
that Jesus freely died on the cross for you.

Which tabernacle do you think Jesus prefers?

Do you think Jesus prefers a tabernacle of gold?

Do you think He prefers the tabernacle
that is you?

I can tell you, without any doubt,
boys and girls, that Jesus prefers the tabernacle
that is YOU
more than any tabernacle of gold or silver.

There is one very special
and
very certain reason why Jesus prefers you.

You can say:

      "Jesus, I love you,"
      when He comes to you.

The golden box cannot talk to Jesus, but you can.
      And
the words Jesus listens for are especially

"Jesus, I love You."

"Jesus, I believe in You."

Jesus comes to you as He did to those two men in the gospel.

They talked with Him, and He talked with them.

And they finally asked, when He was preparing to leave them,

"Lord, stay with us a while."

And Jesus did.

Boys and girls, when Jesus comes to you in Holy Communion,
> talk with Jesus
> tell Jesus you love Him,
> ask Jesus to **stay with you**
> all the days of your life.

Boys and girls, imagine this, if you can:
> All the **angels and saints** in Heaven
> **kneel** before Jesus in heaven.

> That same Jesus is completely and totally
> present in you - the special tabernacle of Jesus today.

> The angels and saints,
> especially your guardian angel and your patron saint,
> would kneel before you for so long
> as Jesus is present in the appearance of bread and wine.

Imagine this - Jesus is the heavens
> and the earth, and He could create
> hundreds and thousands more of everything
> -tiny as a humming bird or big as the night sky.

Jesus is greater than all the universe and yet
> because He loves you and me with a love
> greater than we can imagine,
> Jesus makes himself a prisoner of love in a
>> tabernacle of **gold,**
>> tabernacle of your **little self,**
>>> in a little **bit of bread,**
>>> which **hides** Jesus
>>> to our **eyes,** but **not**
>>> to our **faith** and **love.**

Parents, you bring to church a precious gift today
> -your daughter
> -your son.

You take home **one even more precious-**
one who now has shared for the first time
in the wonder of God's love so precious
and rich that Our Lord says:

"If you eat My flesh and drink My blood
you will live forever."
You **take** home a **living tabernacle.**

Parents, you naturally want the **best** for you son or daughter.

It is *so easy* to give your **child the best-**
bring that one to the Lord's table each Sunday-
Christ pledges to your child **that life is forever**
for those who receive Him
worthily.

Parents, you have the Lord's own invitation and urging.

"Let the little children come to Me."

Enrich your son, your daughter each Sunday
with the **currency that buys heaven.**

It looks like a small coin that
little circle of bread,
but it is really the Risen Lord and Savior,
Jesus, Son of God and Son of Mary.

It is **Jesus' answer** to the men in the gospel
"Stay with us a while."

If it is not, then I say, let us quit,
blow out the candles,
and
go home.

But if it is true, and we are more privileged
than the angels,
more rich in the **riches which last,**
than the richest person in the world
who has only property and money of this world.

Those riches are only for a time.
The riches which come to the First Communicant
and to all who receive the Lord worthily today -
those are forever.

Parents, your children live and will grow up in a
world devoted to secular goals.

Give your precious gifts, your children, your own
inner pledge to give yourself to the project of
unmasking for them the shallowness of
secular values and the depth of catholic principles for
their lives.

Secular values urge us to **feel** good.
Christian principles urge us **to be** good.

And in the end, **to be good** is much more
important than merely **feeling good.**

And to *be good,* your child and you must come to Jesus
at least weekly.
Parents and child must learn to say,

"Lord, stay with us."